"*Light On The Mountain* is literature at the service of Truth, it is a fascinating book."

OUR SUNDAY VISITOR

"You will want to read this book at one sitting."

AMERICA

"In *Light On The Mountain* Father Kennedy demonstrates again his superb talent. . . . The result is nothing short of a masterpiece of popular religious writing."

VOICE OF ST. JUDE

"The story is told with delightful charm."

THE CATHOLIC MISS

"One should not begin this book after ten o'clock at night, or he will find it hard to turn out the light before midnight."

THE CATHOLIC MIRROR

"In an easy-flowing narrative Father Kennedy details the fascinating history of LaSalette. . . . It is a pleasure to recommend *Light On The Mountain*. . . ."

THE QUEEN'S WORK

LIGHT ON THE MOUNTAIN

The Story of LaSalette

John S. Kennedy

IMAGE BOOKS

A division of Doubleday & Company, Inc.,
Garden City, New York

Image Books edition 1956
by special arrangement with McMullen Books, Inc.

PRINTING HISTORY

McMullen Books Inc. edition published November, 1953
1st printing . . . . November, 1953
2nd printing . . . . January, 1954

Image Books edition published March, 1956

Cover by John Carlis
Typography by Edward Gorey

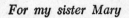

For my sister Mary

The author wishes to express his thanks to Miss Patricia Woods, Mrs. Julia Bossidy and Miss Mary Moran for their work on the manuscript.

Nihil Obstat: Michael J. Cox, M.S.
Censor deputatus

Imprimatur: ✠ *Henry J. O'Brien, D.D.*
Archbishop of Hartford

September 24, 1953

Introduction

The Queen of Heaven in earnest converse with shabby peasant children—this is a picture which Christendom recognizes, and to which it immediately gives the name of Fatima or Lourdes. Another name with the same connotation deserves to be as familiar. It is that of LaSalette, a hamlet in the French Alps, where, in 1846, our Lady appeared to Melanie Mathieu and Maximin Giraud, a pair of small cowherds.

As at Lourdes and Fatima, she had a message and a warning to be communicated to the world by unlikely-looking agents. Indeed, the message and the warning were practically identical on all three occasions. Why, then, is LaSalette much less renowned than Lourdes or Fatima? The reasons are many, of which some may be instanced offhand.

As for Lourdes, it will be remembered that the apparitions there occurred a few years after the solemn definition, in 1854, by Pope Pius IX, of the dogma of Mary's Immaculate Conception. The whole world had been roused by this declaration, a large part of it in enthusiasm, a large part of it in opposition. In either case, our Lady was just then the focus of acute attention, and when the luminous figure at Lourdes spoke the words, "I am the Immaculate Conception," the effect was sure to be electrifying.

Besides, the child favored at Lourdes, Bernadette Soubirous, went on to extraordinary sanctity and eventual canonization. Also, the place itself, readily accessible, became a principal point of pilgrimage for the Catholics of every nation and the scene of countless and often prodigious miracles.

As for Fatima, the extraordinary happenings there are of our own time. For their year is 1917, in the midst of that first World War which, we see in retrospect, was the dividing line between an era of comparative tranquility and stability and one of swift, sweeping, catastrophic change that has loosed horror after horror upon humanity, destroying not merely nations, dynasties, cities, institutions, but also (and more significantly) complacency. In the latter circumstances people are more likely to mark a message and a warning than in the former. Furthermore, Fatima is close by one of the twentieth century's busiest crossroads, Lisbon, a fact facilitating pilgrimage from every quarter.

The story of LaSalette deserves universal notice. It is important in itself, as that of an authentic appearance of the Mother of God. It is important, too, because of the integral link between it, Lourdes, and Fatima.

The circumstances of all three are strikingly similar. The setting, for example, is in each case rural, even primitive, one which bespeaks the difficult lot which falls to most men.

Then, the recipients of an overwhelming favor and mission are children from homes in the withering grip of extreme poverty, children meagerly endowed with talents, intimately acquainted with sorrow and toil, of no consequence by secular standards and without

10

prospects, victims of a prodigal race and an irreligious milieu.

But heaven, we see thrice over, is not unaware of them. Perhaps heaven singles them out as typical of the world's misery which results from the world's waywardness. Certainly heaven singles them out as paradoxically apt instruments for conveying incisive diagnosis of, and sovereign prescription for, the world's deepening misery.

And heaven acts through its Queen, who has a title even more illustrious—Mother.

Mary is the Mother of Jesus Christ, Son of God, who without impairment of His divine nature took to His divine Person a human nature in which to work the redemption of Adam's fallen children. She is, therefore, the Mother of God. She is as well the Mother of the Mystical Body of Christ, of all who are His members, in whatever age and of whatever condition.

It is the mark of the mother to be solicitous for her children. Nor does she ever lay aside her solicitude like a garment outworn. So that Mary in glory is still profoundly concerned for the well-being of her children, and more powerful than ever in coming to their aid.

This is dramatically evidenced at LaSalette, as at Lourdes and Fatima, and, it should be observed, at LaSalette before it was at Lourdes and Fatima. She manifested herself to witnesses incapable of imagining or fabricating anything of the sort, witnesses peculiarly receptive and peculiarly qualified to transmit verbatim what it was she wanted said to the world.

And what was that? At LaSalette, Lourdes, Fatima, essentially the same.

First, she stresses the crucial fact of sin, its evil and its sure and swelling consequences. The woes of the world are reducible to this—that men set the will of

11

God at naught and plunge into habitual wrong-doing. But when the commandments are broken, the lives of men are broken no less, and their peace. When the seeds of sin are sown, a crop of troubles and of sufferings inevitably proliferates. And, more than that, divine chastisement in dire forms is laid upon humanity. Cause and effect—this is clarified on all three occasions. A warning is sounded that if the first is not corrected, the second is sure to grow worse.

How accomplish the correction? By two means.

One is prayer. Men must address God, resuming a colloquy they have broken off. To address Him necessitates turning to Him, attending to Him. Intent on Him, they must voice adoration, praise, contrition for sin, petitions for grace. This, sincerely done, means a radical change of heart. It cannot be sincerely done without renunciation of that slavery to sin in which they have been content to wallow. It involves a new orientation—away from what is base and ruinous, to what is supremely good and saving.

And it is followed by a shower, a deluge, of grace. For the mercy of God shines out splendidly on each of these occasions, which concretize His willingness to forgive the penitent and to bless and reward immeasurably those who renounce sin and cleave to Him.

The other means is penance. It was by sacrifice that the world was redeemed. It is in part by sacrifice that men do their share in the attaining of salvation and in helping others to it. Reparation must be made for offenses. The temporal punishment due to sin must be paid off. We must fulfill our obligation, as members of the Mystical Body, to carry the Cross. And to prevent relapse into the ways of deranged nature which have proved our own, and the world's, ruin, we must abide by St. Paul's dictum, "If you live a life of nature, you are marked out for death; if you mortify the ways of nature through the power of the Spirit, you will have life."

In all this, there is nothing new. But men grow heedless. They forget. They are distracted. They sink down into spiritual sloth and apathy. They need prompting as to the principles and laws which govern the relations of heaven and earth and determine the prosperity or adversity obtaining within and among men. When the situation is desperate, when a crisis impends, the prompting has to be especially emphatic. Hence La-Salette. And repetition is required if the situation worsens and the crisis becomes total. Hence Lourdes and then Fatima.

They are all three of a piece, and far more impressive when seen and studied in relationship one to another. It is to make the first better known that this book was written.

1

"Nothing ever happens in this godforsaken place."

It is easy to imagine such words being said by a supercilious traveler stretching his legs in the main square of Corps in the French Alps one day in early September, 1846. The traveler might have had to spend a grudged half-hour in the town because the coach in which he was riding to or from the nearest city, Grenoble, required some minor repair. Corps, poor, backward, with but 1,300 inhabitants, would have little appeal, not even that of picturesqueness, for a citizen of the great world. A dull place, unheard of and readily forgotten.

Had this slighting remark been made to one of the more literate residents of Corps, the traveler might have been rather heatedly told that the section of France where he had the privilege of finding himself did not lack distinction. Take Grenoble, for example. That city, some 50 miles away, dated from the time of the ancient Gauls. The Romans, under Gratian, had fortified it and named it Gratianopolis after the emperor. Not too far distant was the village of Vizille, in whose environs stood the storied chateau of the Duc de Lesdiguières. In that capacious house had met, in 1788, the Assembly of the States General of the Dauphiné, an event commonly regarded as the prelude to the French Revolution of the following year. And what of Laffrey, another village in the vicinity? Had the traveler never heard of what took place there in 1815? The great Napoleon, escaped from Elba and making his way toward Paris with an insignificant number of supporters, encountered at Laffrey the picked troops dispatched from the capital to find and arrest him. The former emperor had walked alone toward the guns and the clouded faces, said a few words as only he could, and instantly turned his would-be captors into a cheering escort for his triumphal journey to one hundred days of glory.

Moreover, there was the scenery. Where would one find its like? The mountains in majestic array as far as one could see, giant after giant proudly thrusting against the sky, the loftiest gleaming with snow which defied the relentless sun. The plateaus, green and stone-strewn, where cows and goats were pastured. The quiet valleys. The sharply pitched gorges. The rivers and crystal streams pursuing their sinuous courses. Beautiful country, and not in the least insipid.

"Scenery," the traveler with citified tastes might have sniffed. "As for the great doings you boast of, they are of the moldering past. Napoleon came through here thirty-one years ago, did he? Well, since then we have had two Bourbon kings, another revolution, and the Orléans monarchy which probably won't last much longer. Or maybe, in your stagnant backwater, you hadn't heard? I still say that nothing ever happens in this godforsaken place." The coach repaired, he would have climbed in with alacrity, gladly heard the author-

16

itative crack of the driver's whip, gladly left frowzy, depressing Corps behind.

Truth to tell, whether or not one was a stranger, it was an unprepossessing place, with its huddle of grey, grim-looking houses, its narrow streets, its old, weather-beaten, desolate-seeming church. For all that the church dominated the town, this was no godly place. Few were the people who went to any of the services. Sunday Mass drew a handful. The dust in the confessional, on the communion rail, was undisturbed.

Many factors would figure in an explanation of this situation. Ancient abuses and grievances still festered. The Revolution had fostered irreligion, and popular confusion as to who were, and who were not, priests in good standing. Since the Revolution there had been conflict between Church and government, with an inevitable bad effect on the people. Fierce talk about the rights of man had filtered down to the common folk as meaning the canceling out of duties owed to God. A narrow, necessitous existence had served to harden hearts, encrusting them with crude materialism. Then, there had been that scandalous business of the unworthy pastor whom the bishop of the Grenoble diocese had suspended. The offender refused to submit, and roused his partisans to defy and humiliate his duly appointed successor. Those had been exciting days, when the new priest was hooted at and grossly insulted in the streets and loudly told to leave. But he had stayed, and the quarrel had subsided, not without leaving rifts, scars.

No wonder, then, that cursing and swearing were heard on every side, even in the piping voices of children, or that blasphemies singed the very air, or that everyone toiled all through Sunday as if it were no different from the rest of the week. Fast and abstinence?

They were paid no heed. After work, the dingy, fetid cabarets were crowded, pouring into the night shrieks of laughter, raucous singing, the clamor of crapulous quarreling, as one or another patron pushed open the door and staggered into the dark. Well might the mountains look down with disdain. God-forgotten Corps was not; no place is. But Corps could be said to have forgotten—or almost forgotten—God.

Take that man headed for the café. Giraud. Giraud was a wheelwright and something of a carpenter, the only one in town. He had work enough to keep him occupied, with farmers requiring repairs to their vehicles, and with coaches from the highway in need of attention after mile upon jolting mile. Giraud, however busy, was poor. And much of what little money he laid hands on he left in the cabarets. He took delight in his reputation as one of the heaviest drinkers in Corps. No one would put him under the table.

No more would anyone in need of his services find him in church. Between workshop and drinkshop, he had no time for church-going. He was at home very little. The small, dark stone house was confining and cheerless. His first wife had died, and he had married again. His second choice was not altogether a happy one. Not a bad woman, she seems to have been a nagger. And what man can put up with a nagger, especially when he thoroughly deserves to be nagged?

By his first wife Giraud had a daughter and a son. The latter, Maximin, eleven years old in 1846, was not fond of his stepmother, whose affection was monopolized by the children she bore Giraud. She was hardly a paragon of kindness and patience, often failing to feed the boy, yet she may have had reason to be vexed with him. He was good-looking, though not very tall for his age. "Eleven years old?" people would say incredulously. "Why, he looks no more than eight, and a puny eight at that." But the child was healthy, as the ruddy color of his smudged face showed. Roving black eyes, under his tousled hair, truly indicated his character. He was lively and inquisitive, impetuous and pert. His attention never stayed fixed for long; he could not concentrate; he darted about ceaselessly, tirelessly, and so did his mind. His undependability, even frivolity, may understandably have annoyed his step-mother and evoked those reproofs and complaints which he sought to avoid by staying away from home.

He spent his time mostly in play, in games strenuous and noisy, in throwing stones at any target. He roamed the town at will, early and late, his mongrel dog Loulou tagging at his heels. Sometimes, though, he had jobs to do. He collected dung along the heavily traveled highway. Or he kept an eye on the family's goat and ewe. Giraud, proud of his trade and considering himself no bumpkin since he had seen other parts of France, took it for granted that the boy would follow that trade and may have occasionally given him a demonstration of how this or that task was done. But for the most part, he paid Maximin little notice. He never sent him to school; before 1846, Maximin had spent not even an hour in a classroom. He could not read. He knew a word or two of French, but spoke a patois.

Nor did his father take him to church. His grandmother, concerned about the lad, probably was the person who brought Maximin to church now and again. But always he managed to slip away, with the Mass scarcely begun, to rejoin his playmates at some boisterous pursuit out in the sunny square where the men lounged conspicuously while services lasted. Despite his carelessness about religion and his preoccupation with work or pleasure, the father, perhaps remembering his first wife, made spasmodic attempts to teach her son some prayers. After four years of such intermittent coaching, the boy could stumble through the "Our Father" and the "Hail Mary."

If Giraud did not take Maximin to church, he did take him along to the café. And there, for the amusement of his cronies, he endeavored to train the little lad in drinking and smoking. The ignorant, neglected Maximin would have some accomplishments.

A miserable existence, you might say. Maximin would later so style it. But then, in this town where nothing ever happened, there did happen something which had astonishing consequences.

On Sunday, September 13, 1846, there came into Corps one Pierre Selme. Selme was a farmer with a place higher up in the mountains. He was from La-Salette, a parish comprising some half-dozen hamlets, one of which was Ablandins, where Selme lived. The farmer employed a child to look after his four cows. Daily the cows were taken out to graze in Selme's mountain meadow. They had to be constantly watched, for in their wanderings they might easily fall into a ravine if not headed away from dangerous spots. Selme's herder had become ill. It was necessary to get a replacement at once.

In his search he encountered Giraud. He was already acquainted with the wheelwright. Selme asked Giraud to let Maximin substitute for a week. Giraud, solemn and touchy in his drink, was inclined to think it beneath the dignity of a son of his to do a herder's work. The boy was to be an artisan, not a rustic handyman. Wasn't the very suggestion insulting? We can see the liquored indignation in the face of the always hard-up, always frustrated man who has not parted with his pride. Selme was persistent, persuasive. Very well, Giraud would set the terms. The boy would take along the family goat and supervise its grazing on Selme's land. Selme would keep the boy in sight all the time (something which Giraud himself never did). Maximin would be brought home the following Sunday without fail, carrying with him his wages and, as additional payment for his service, an abundant supply of butter and cheese. Agreed, said the desperate Selme. Giraud could sit back, pleased with this exhibition of proper pride, paternal solicitude, and skill in bargaining.

So, on Monday, accompanied by his dog and the family goat, Maximin went, for a week, to the town of Ablandins in the parish of LaSalette. There he was to meet another youngster from Corps, Melanie Mathieu, a fourteen-year-old girl whom, despite the smallness of Corps, he had not previously known.

Their being unacquainted with each other was hardly surprising. Melanie was from a family even needier than Maximin's, and lived at the other end of town during the short scattered periods when she was at home. There were eight children in that wretchedly poor household from which the cloud of harassment never lifted. Merely to get a little to eat was a ceaseless struggle. When she was very small, Melanie's parents sent her into the streets to beg. She began to work when she was seven or eight. At first she minded babies, now for one family, now for another. Before she was ten, she was hired out as farm help from March to December. For two years she took care of the cows of a farmer at Quet-en-Beaumont. For another two years she did the same work at Sainte-Luce. Later, she served at Saint-Michel. In March, 1846, she had been engaged by Baptiste Pra of Ablandins, and daily thereafter she guided his small herd to his piece of pasturage in the mountains, adjoining that of Pierre Selme. She was by now, we are told, a professional herder, and not, like Maximin, an amateur. She had status.

A pitiable figure, this one dignified as a professional. She too was undersize, a runty specimen, plain and pale and anything but robust. She was a silent child; some thought her sulky. Certainly she was timid, fearful. But had she not reason to be so? Of love, of kindness, she had known little; much less of security. Is begging in the streets, whatever the weather, calculated to make a child gay and carefree? From an early age Melanie had had almost no home life, no enjoyment of family affection. Her parents, though poor providers, had more regard for their children than was ever expended on Maximin. But there were so many of the Mathieus swarming in the gloomy house, so much to be done, so little to do with, and always the dread of stark starvation was so pressing.

For nine months of the year Melanie lived away from home, and her employers were grasping people, without a trace of sentimentality. In their eyes she was not a child to be cherished, but a chattel to be worked to the utmost, fed and paid as little as possible. In their homes she was a stranger, a shadow without personality, left to her own devices, often sleeping in the stable with the beasts she tended, or sometimes, on summer nights, out under the impassive stars. Her clothes, if wet from a deluge on the mountain, she wore while they dried; no one showed any anxiety about her. She was a child who had had no childhood, a child deprived, like Maximin, of a mother's close, indulgent attention.

But 1846 had already brought her a measure of

blessing in the mother of that Baptiste Pra who was now employing Melanie. Wrinkled Grandmother Pra evidenced some interest in the uncommunicative, hard-worked girl who spent lonely days on the mountain and then, at dusk, returned to milk and bed down the cows, to gulp her bowl of soup, and to fall exhausted on her makeshift bed. "But, child," said the old woman, "you hardly ever say your prayers! You'll see, one of these days a devil or something of the sort will be along to carry you off."

What prayers did Melanie, who had had not a day's schooling, know? The "Our Father" and the "Hail Mary" in patois, for she had just scraps of French. These prayers her mother had taught her, that perpetually worried woman who distractedly wondered what would ever become of her scrawny little ones. A few bits of the catechism, too, Mme. Mathieu had drilled into her daughter at long intervals. But they were no more than odd bits, which Melanie could repeat only laboriously and understood hardly at all. She had been to church but a few times in her life. Wasn't there the begging to be done, or the duty demanded by close-fisted employers who considered Sunday simply another day of work? Fourteen years old, almost fifteen, and she had not yet made her first Communion. How could she have? That had to be prepared for, at length, in catechism classes conducted by the curé of Corps, M. Mélin, and he had not so much as set eyes on this professional herder, generally so far from home.

But Melanie did have some vague ideas about the saints. In her few visits to church, she had noticed their shadowy statues. And as, with her few, shabby possessions in a crumpled bundle, she walked the country roads to Quet-en-Beaumont or Sainte-Luce or Saint-Michel or wherever the new job waited, and as she brought the dawdling cows to pasture and back, she sometimes saw a shrine along the way. These, too, were reminders of the saints. Precisely what saints were, what they did, what they meant, she could not say. At any rate, they were great personages, remote, unearthly, beyond her horizon.

Such were the children from Corps who, on Thursday evening, September 17, 1846, met for the first time. Maximin told Melanie that he was usually called Mémin, and introduced his frisky dog Loulou. On Friday they tended their cows, Melanie in Pra's meadow, Maximin in Selme's nearby property on the mountain. As the sun declined, they came down to the town together, driving the cows before them, with Maximin doing most of the talking, and Melanie at least a little reluctant to chatter and laugh with one whom she hardly knew and didn't much care for. Chatting and laughing she was unversed in, anyhow. She had had little practice in either. As they parted, one said to the other, "Tomorrow we'll go back to the mountain. We'll see who'll be the first up." The smiling challenge certainly was voiced by Maximin. Tomorrow, back to the mountain. A day like any other. The same uneventful routine. "Nothing ever happens in this godforsaken place."

2

The hamlet of Ablandins was still drowned in darkness when, early on Saturday, September 19, Maximin's shouts and mocking laughter outside Pra's door awakened those within. He was up before Melanie, to the shame of the professional herder. She must hurry to dress (no time for praying even on this ember day, the eve of the Feast of Our Lady of Sorrows), to have a bit of breakfast, to throw together the lunch she would take with her, to rout the cows out of the dingy stable and set them on their way. How the capering Maximin jeered at her as, finally, she was ready to start for the mountain meadows. A bad beginning for Melanie's day.

Pierre Selme had been as good as his word to Maximin's father. He or his wife, shaking their heads over the lad's irresponsibility and telling each other that they would be glad if their regular herder was well enough to resume work sooner than expected, had always kept Maximin in sight. It was hard for Selme, trying to cut hay up there on the mountain, to have to stop at short intervals, shade his eyes against the sunlight, and look to see where the boy had got to now and what he was up to. A pesky lad, he had not even bothered to master the simple routine required of him. Always he had to be reminded of what he should do next. The poor beasts might perish of thirst for all Maximin noticed.

There he was at the door, hopping on one foot, then the other, as Melanie came out. His rough breeches were topped by a soiled white smock. His long, rumpled hair sprang out every which way, Medusa-like. He carried a thick staff, twirling his large felt hat around and around on the end of it. Melanie was wearing a dress of homespun, full-skirted and reaching to her boots. It covered her arms to the wrists, and over it was an apron, in the local fashion. Her thin, neatly molded face was framed by a white cap tied under the chin. She, too, had a stout staff; it was the herder's badge of office and kept the cows moving when they would rather tarry over a choice bit at the wayside.

All present and accounted for now: the children, the eight cows, the one goat, and Loulou. And here was Selme, his scythe over his shoulder, ready for another day's mowing. It was time to start.

The street was still thronged with twilight as the party moved off. When they reached the edge of town, they looked up at Mt. Obiou, the peak which outsoared all others thereabouts, beginning to glitter as it caught the sun. Would they or anyone ever see a sight more thrilling? It would be a good day for Selme's haying and for the children's long stay in the open. Mountain after mountain sprang again into formidable being from the once-obliterating dusk. The sky was flooded with light, quickened to a dazzling blue. A chill edged the air, but soon there would be warmth enough.

Meanwhile, there was the brisk exercise involved in ordering the cows forward. Maximin was clowning with his dog, giving her fantastic commands, throwing sticks to be retrieved, and all the while laughing uproariously. How tiresome this boy could be, for one of Melanie's serious and even a little melancholy disposition. But she, like Selme, might console herself with the thought that tomorrow the unsatisfactory substitute went back home. Thereafter he and she would have nothing to do with each other, for no bond would hold them.

Up, up they moved, turning here to skirt a steep ravine in which a torrent foamed, there to avoid a patch of vegetation which might detain the cows. At last they had reached the fields of Selme and Pra. It was smiling morning. The children could settle down to their monotonous vigil, each in a different field. The fragrance of freshly cut grass was wafted to them as Selme's scythe rhythmically flashed.

September. The golden month. Summer gone, autumn ripening, and rumors of winter in occasional winds from the glaciers. Melanie, sitting pensively on a rock, could think of her return home in a matter of weeks. Were things any better there? Would she find a happier, less harried household beyond the mean doorway? Hardly likely. She would be bringing home about seventy francs, her wages for nine months' work. Seventy francs would not go far in the cold months of idleness. How terrible that no one cared for such as the Mathieus. No apprehensive thoughts for Maximin, playing by himself, frolicking with Loulou, concerned only about one of Selme's cows, Red by name, of which, for all his bravado, he was afraid. So, emptily, passed the morning.

Suddenly, faintly but in silver tones, the Angelus bell rang out across the distance. In the belfry of LaSalette church someone was tugging at the well-worn rope and sending through the mountains the ancient, heartening assurance, "The angel of the Lord declared unto Mary, and she conceived of the Holy Spirit. Hail Mary, full of grace . . . Mother of God, pray for us sinners." It was noon. Selme straightened from his labors and shouted to Maximin, but his was no summons to prayer. "Mémin, quick, quick, go water the cows!"

"I'll get Melanie," was the reply, "and the two of us will go to the fountain together."

The fountain so-called was one of three drinking places in the nearby ravine, named la Sézia after the stream which ran through it. The ravine was a curving depression of no great depth, easy for children and animals to negotiate. The cows would drink at a spring known as the fountain of the beasts. A second was known as the men's fountain, and alongside it dead and forgotten generations of herders had eaten lunch, seated on rocks arranged like chairs around a large, flat rock which served as a table. Between the two was a third source, called "the little fountain," which gave water only after heavy snows or rains, and now was utterly dry.

One by one the cows drank their fill, each greedy creature in turn having to be driven off so that the others might have a chance. The watering done, Melanie and Maximin could open their knapsacks and have their frugal meal, country bread and cheese, washed down with cold water. They relished it after the long morning in the tangy air. As they ate and drank, throwing scraps to the begging Loulou, they were joined for a few minutes by three other herders, one of them, Rosette de la Minouna, a girl from Corps. She was surprised to find Maximin Giraud here. Mémin tending cows? What an idea! For whom? For how long? He had come only last Monday? Well, then, he could give her news of Corps, and, when he returned tomorrow, he could bring her family a message from her. He mightn't remember it? At least let him tell them that he had seen her. Agreed. The three moved on.

How warm it was, now at the day's zenith, under the proudly regnant sun. How lulling was the sweetness of flower and herb in their last flourishing. The children, who had been up so early, felt drowsy. They lay down upon the ground, near the dried-up fountain. In a speeding minute they were asleep, the remnants of their lunch beside them. For the first time one could see Melanie's face emptied of care, Maximin's face in repose. The writing of difficult or feckless years was erased from each innocent page.

Almost two hours of silence passed in this place, so far above the world, so serene, where no bird call was ever heard, where great events were not even echoed, and no one of any importance had ever set foot.

Melanie started up, her face flushed with sleep, her practised eye at once recognizing that considerable time had elapsed. Was not the sun noticeably farther west? And where were the cows? Not a sign of them. "Mémin," the girl shouted at the still sleeping Maximin, "Mémin, get up at once. We must go look for the cows. I don't know where they are." Her solicitude for their charges communicated itself to the boy. Blinking, rubbing his eyes, he went after her, then turned to snatch up his staff so as to be able to deal with the beasts, especially the ugly Red.

Once they had hurried up the side of the ravine, they could see the cows grazing tranquilly on another flank of the mountain, all eight of them, with the goat trailing after. What a relief! Melanie turned back toward the ravine. Enough of dalliance. The knapsacks in which they had carried their lunch must be retrieved. Then it would be time to water the animals once again. The day was running out with the westering sun. With determined strides the girl hurried toward the ravine. At its edge, she suddenly, transfixedly, stopped.

In the ravine, only a few feet away, there blazed a great circle of light. It was like the sun, yet even more brilliant and of a different color. The astounded child looked at it wide-eyed, looked away, looked back. It was still there.

"Mémin," she shrilly called to the boy, who she knew had been following her. "Mémin, come quickly; see the light shining down there."

He was at her heels. "Where is it," he asked.

"There," she pointed.

To his stupefaction, he saw it, too.

"O my God," cried the now terribly frightened Melanie, and as she did so, the staff slipped from her trembling hand and fell clattering on the stones.

"Hold onto that staff of yours," Maximin told her, "and I will hold onto mine, and if *that* attempts to hurt us, I will give it a hard whack." His father's son, this young Giraud.

Before their fascinated gaze the light grew in splendor, became ever more dazzling. The children put their hands before their eyes for respite, then looked again, only to be further alarmed by its swelling intensity. They would have fled, dashing pell mell down the mountain, cows and goat forgotten, had they not just then noticed something happening to the incredibly effulgent globe. It was opening up, and the children could, little by little, discern within it the figure of a woman, defined by a still more exquisite radiance. The woman was seated, bent forward. Her face was bowed in her hands. Her elbows rested on her knees. She was weeping. How strange, yet how compelling, the glory and the tears.

Who was she?

"O my God," again burst from Melanie, for she had remembered Grandmother Pra's warning that some devil would yet waylay her and carry her off because of her neglect of prayer. It had come true, then, that dire prophecy. Maximin, meanwhile, was thinking simple-mindedly that this weeping woman must be a mother whose children had struck her and who had come away to the mountain solitude and seated herself on the rock at the dry fountain to cry her heart out.

The luminous figure now arose, her head inclined a little to one side, her arms crossed upon her breast. The beauty of the face, seen clearly by Melanie but not by Maximin, was extraordinary, despite the ceaselessly falling tears. A lucent white headdress covered the woman's hair, clung to her cheeks, hid her neck. A towering crown rested on her brow, edged below with roses of many colors which gave off shimmering rays of light. A long white dress, with ample sleeves and sprinkled with bursts of light in the shape of pearls, clothed the figure in splendor. Upon the woman's shoulders and crossed upon her breast was a small shawl, blindingly white and trimmed with roses which seemed to form golden lace. Along the hem of the shawl were ranged metal links, not joined in a chain, but distinctly separated one from the next. Tied about her waist was a large apron, yellow and glittering as gold. Her feet were shod in white slippers decorated with clusters of pearls, gold buckles, and the same scintillant sort of roses as those on crown and shawl. Upon her breast was a crucifix, depending from a chain. The figure on the cross was as of fire. To the left of the crucifix was a hammer; to the right, a pair of pliers, half-open: the tools, respectively, with which the nails were fixed in, then withdrawn from, the Saviour's hands on Calvary.

Gazing at this lustrous apparition, the children were dumbfounded, in the grip of both enchantment and consternation. Then the woman spoke, in a voice of surpassing gentleness, its sound as soothing as commanding. It fell upon the children's ears with a power to attract, penetrate, reassure, such as no other voice had ever exerted upon them.

"Come to me, my children," the woman said, in French. "Do not be afraid. I am here to tell you something of the greatest importance."

The fright, unaccustomedly mixed with delight, which had held the children rigid, melted. They stepped forward, descending the side of the ravine, crossing the bed of the stream. The woman, all queenly graciousness, moved to meet them. In a moment they were so close to her that they could have touched her. No one could have passed between them and her. They found themselves enveloped in the globe of light; light so bright that it offset that of the sun and swallowed up their shadows. Alert, expectant, Melanie at her right, Maximin at her left, they looked up to the ineffably glowing face, the glorious eyes from which crystalline tears fell constantly. What was it she had to tell them?

Again she spoke, the sound from her lips like music, but the sense ominous. "If my people will not obey," she said, "I shall be compelled to loose my Son's arm. It is so heavy, so pressing that I can no longer restrain it. How long have I suffered for you! If my Son is not to cast you off, I am obliged to entreat Him without ceasing. But you take no least heed of that. No matter how well you pray in future, no matter how well you act, you will never be able to make up to me what I have endured in your behalf.

"I have appointed you six days for working. The seventh I have reserved for myself. And no one will give it to me. This it is which causes the weight of my Son's arm to be so crushing.

"The cart drivers cannot swear without bringing in my Son's name. These are the two things which make my Son's arm so burdensome.

"If the harvest is spoiled, it is your own fault. I warned you last year by means of the potatoes. You paid no attention. Quite the reverse, when you discovered that the potatoes had decayed, you swore, you abused my Son's name. They will continue to be spoiled, and by Christmas time this year there will be none left."

Melanie tore her eyes from the magnetic face and looked inquiringly at Maximin. There was much here which she did not understand, for the woman spoke in French and Melanie's knowledge of that language was rudimentary. Without waiting to see what the boy would do, the woman said, "Ah, you do not understand French, my children. Well then, listen. I shall put it differently." Then, in the local patois, she repeated what she had already said.

She went on, "If you have grain, it will do no good to sow it, for what you sow the beasts will eat, and whatever part of it springs up will crumble into dust when you thresh it.

"A great famine is coming. But before that happens, the children under seven years of age will be seized with trembling and die in the arms of the parents holding them. The grownups will pay for their sins by hunger. The grapes will rot and the walnuts will turn bad."

33

The woman broke off her recital of reproaches and threats, and turned to Maximin. She spoke to him at some length, but not a word that she said could Melanie catch, although the girl could see the woman's lips moving. Melanie's childhood experience told her what this was: a secret for Maximin. Then the woman turned to her and confided a secret which Maximin, strain though he might, could not hear.

The discourse was resumed, on a different note. "If people are converted, the rocks will become piles of wheat and it will be found that the potatoes have sown themselves."

Another break. Looking searchingly at the poor, shabbily clad youngsters, so early put to work, the woman asked, "Do you say your prayers well, my children?" Maximin kicked at a stone. "No, Madame," he joined Melanie in saying, "hardly at all."

"Ah, my children, it is very important to do so, at night and in the morning. When you don't have time, at least say an 'Our Father' and a 'Hail Mary,' and when you can, say more."

Another return to the main theme. "Only a few rather old women go to Mass in the summer. Everyone else works every Sunday all summer long. And in winter, when they don't know what to do with themselves, they go to Mass only to scoff at religion. During Lent, they go to the butcher shop like dogs."

Then another question. "My children, haven't you ever seen spoiled wheat?"

"No, Madame," Maximin replied, "we never have."

She looked squarely at him. "But you, my child, must have seen it once, near Coin, with your papa. The owner of a field said to your papa, 'Come and see my spoiled wheat.' The two of you went. You took two or three ears of wheat in your hands. You rubbed them,

34

and they crumbled to dust. Then you came back from Coin. When you were only a half-hour away from Corps, your papa gave you a bit of bread and said, 'Well, my son, eat some bread this year, anyhow. I don't know who'll be eating any next year if the wheat continues to spoil like that.'"

As she said this, Maximin recalled the incident. Amazing that this woman knew of it in such detail, knew even what his father had said to him when the two of them were entirely alone on the road. Maximin had not thought of that conversation since, nor had his father ever referred to it. But this woman had it word for word. Awe-struck, he answered, "It's very true, Madame. Now I remember it. Until now I didn't."

The woman again resorted to French. "Well, my children, you will make this known to all my people." These were her last words. She concluded as unexpectedly as she had begun. Her final remark was plainly a command, but she did not specify how it was to be carried out. That was for them to determine.

She turned from them now, slowly but unmistakably. Maximin moved aside to let her do so. She stepped across the stream bed, then paused and, without looking back at them, repeated the charge she had laid upon them, "Well, my children, you will make this known to all my people."

Slowly she walked the length of the ravine, up the slope which led to higher ground. The children, enthralled, accompanied her, Melanie a little ahead, Maximin a little behind. The boy feared that, walking, she would crush the roses with which the soles of her slippers were outlined. But no! She glided, above the ground, so that the grass did not even bend as she passed. At the top of the ravine she paused. Gracefully she rose into the air. She looked up to heaven, a long, joyous moment this, during which, for the only time since the children had first seen her, she ceased to weep. Then another look out over the world, her glance directed to the southeast, toward Rome. She, and the circle of light surrounding her, shone with yet greater brilliance. She began to disappear. With a cry of protest, of yearning, Maximin reached out to grasp the incomparable light, the flowers on the woman's feet. In vain. The apparition faded into the upper air, leaving a path of radiance which, in a few seconds, vanished without trace.

3

For some minutes they continued to look upward, in mute longing. They did not stir, lest the transporting happiness which had swept over them as soon as the woman began to speak be dissipated. It had lifted them out of the drab round which, despite the natural grandeur crowding the horizon, was their environment since birth. Nobility, majesty, magnanimity, loveliness, of such they had known nothing, but now, for a little while, had known everything. Were these again to be entirely lost to them, along with her who had exemplified them?

At length the children looked at each other, the one reading in the other's eyes the evidence of glory seen, of wonders heard. Melanie sighed. "Perhaps," she said finally, dreamily, "perhaps she was a great saint." Doubtless the child was thinking of the figures, with haloes dimmed by grime or weathering, which she had seen in church or wayside shrine.

"If we had known she was a great saint," Maximin replied, "we should have asked her to take us with her." Did the word "heaven," so unthinkingly mouthed as he gropingly repeated the "Our Father" at Giraud's

37

sporadic insistence, now have a brighter spark of meaning?

"Oh, if only she were still here," said Melanie, who had known so little tenderness, so little kindling of mind and heart, for whom everything had always been so dull, so grindingly hard. And then, "She didn't want us to watch her any longer, so that we should not see where it was she went." No, not a flicker of the idea of heaven here.

Well, back to the job. Time had passed, perhaps half an hour, since the two had first seen the globe of light in the ravine. The cows and the goat must be rounded up, watered again, driven home. The knapsacks were still to be retrieved. The children set out after the animals. In the distance, like specks in the vast, overpowering landscape, the three herders with whom they had chatted for a few minutes at noon could be seen. Yes, the workaday world had reclaimed them now, and on it, in all likelihood, the marvel on the mountain would make as much impression as writing on water.

"Say," Maximin suddenly exclaimed, glancing sharply at Melanie, "once she stopped talking, but I saw her keep on moving her lips. What did she say?"

The childishly sly maneuver failed. "She told me something," Melanie answered, "but I won't tell it to you. She told me not to."

"Oh, that doesn't bother me," said Maximin. "She told me something, too, but I'm not going to let you in on it, either."

As they approached the cows, each thought of the secret solemnly imparted and to be scrupulously kept. No sign of Selme. He had finished his haying and started back to the town. For some minutes the children were occupied with forcing the cows to leave off grazing and move toward the fountain of the beasts.

"How beautiful she was," Maximin said as they fell in step behind the ambling cows. "Do you know what I thought the prettiest thing about her? Her cross."

"The most brilliant things were her shawl, her chain, and her cross. But if she had given me a dress like hers," said the girl who had always worn nondescript clothes, "or even one not quite so pretty, I'd certainly have taken it."

In the now lonesome ravine they found Loulou. What an odd thing that this dog, always bustling about and barking, always bristling and growling at strangers, had been silent, motionless, indeed asleep all the time that the resplendent woman had stood before them and talked to them. Another indication that, whoever she was, she was no ordinary person.

They picked up their knapsacks, shouted at the cows, dealt them a few blows, and the homeward descent began. Certainly the town would be ringing with excitement, for the woman enwrapped in fire must have been seen there, if only from afar. They did their best to speed the slow-gaited beasts. But in Ablandins there reigned the wonted quiet of early evening, when smoke rose from the chimneys like plumes against the sunset sky and supper was put piping on the table and the stools were dragged across the flagged floor and everyone, weary and hungry, fell to, without a word. The disappointed children parted.

Selme was standing in the doorway when Maximin came in sight. "You're late," he told the boy, relieved that nothing untoward had happened and voicing his relief in the paradoxical but usual way of reproach. "Why didn't you come back to the field after watering the cows, as you did every other day?"

Maximin answered that he and Melanie had been detained by a woman.

39

Detained by a woman? Stuff and nonsense, a poor, transparent semblance of an excuse! Did he think that Selme would be taken in by a clumsy lie like that?

But they *had* been. "Near the stream bed we came upon a beautiful lady who detained us for a long time. I was afraid at first. I didn't dare to go get my bread which was near where she was. But then she said, 'Come to me, my children. Don't be afraid. I am here to tell you great news.'" Thus launched, Maximin poured out the whole story, as Selme, reluctant to credit it but deeply impressed by the boy's rapt manner, listened in grave, troubled silence. Was this a taradiddle to divert attention from yet another failure, another act of disobedience on the part of the amateur herder? Selme would soon find out. After supper they would go to Pra's house, and he would question Melanie, that sober, steady youngster who spoke no foolishness.

Maximin was at Pra's ahead of his employer. He bolted his supper and dashed through the street. But Melanie was not in the low-ceilinged kitchen with the rest of the household when the boy opened the door. She was still in the stable, readying the cows for the night, a task which Selme did not require of Maximin.

"Didn't any of you see a beautiful lady surrounded by fire pass through the air?"

What was this? Soup spoons arrested, they all looked at him. Was he in earnest? Yes, indeed. Hadn't any of them noticed the light blazing on the mountain this afternoon? What was he talking about? He began the story all over again, while the older people curiously watched his shining face and were moved in spite of their native skepticism and their distrust of this flighty lad.

When he had done, Grandmother Pra got up

quickly. She had perceived what these racing words might mean. She would find and question Melanie. The short, slim girl could hardly be seen in the dark stable. "Melanie," the old woman called, "leave the cows. I'll see to them later. Come and tell us what it was you saw with Mémin."

So he was spreading the news already. "Oh well," Melanie said, "whatever I saw with Mémin he has already told you, and you know it." But she obeyed Grandmother Pra nonetheless. Into the house she went, to face the family, with Maximin in their midst, talking all at once around the table. She, too, told the story, from the first detail to the last, and her account agreed perfectly with what they had just heard.

"You see, then," Grandmother Pra cried, shaking a knobby forefinger at her son. "You hear what the Blessed Virgin said to this child? I suppose you're still going to work tomorrow—it's Sunday, remember—after that!"

"Bah," her son answered. "Do you think I'm going to believe that the likes of this one saw the Blessed Virgin? Why, she doesn't even say her prayers!"

The Blessed Virgin. It was Grandmother Pra who first identified the beautiful lady. Neither of the children had given her a name. Neither had realized who she was, even after what she had said of her Son. Nor had Selme drawn, or at least voiced, the obvious conclusion. But the old farm woman, hearing the recital of the event a first time, a second time, and marking every word, portentous or benign, spoken by the radiant stranger, recognized the truth.

By this time Selme had arrived, and with him and after him came other people of Ablandins, for the news had flown from house to house. The kitchen was crowded, the talk clamorous and incessant. Again and

41

again the boy and the girl were questioned, he taking all this attention and stir with delight, she with distaste. It was eventually decided that this was something to be submitted to the Church. Hence, first thing in the morning, the children should go off to LaSalette and tell their story to the pastor, Father Jacques Perrin, who was shortly to leave for another parish at St. Sixte, but was still in charge of LaSalette. Hold on. Maximin had to go home tomorrow, didn't he? Selme had promised Giraud. No trouble about that; Selme could take the boy to Corps after the interview with Father Perrin. Very well.

The kitchen quieted, emptied. Grandmother Pra went in to have a look at Melanie, to see that the child was all right after the day's marvel and the night's debate. Lamp in hand, she stood in amazement at the door. The lamplight showed Melanie on her knees, her eyes closed, her hands joined. She was praying, as that afternoon she had been told to pray. She was praying a long time, she who knew so little of the words, the forms of prayer. The old woman smiled. "Praying, are you, and at great length? I suppose it's to make up for all the times when you didn't."

She put the girl to bed. But Melanie's rest was only in snatches, and the Pras, through the still darkness, could hear her talking in her sleep. "What should I do? What should I do? How am I going to make it known to all the people?" The charge given her had penetrated to the depths of her being. She would not forget it.

As for Maximin, his was the bland sleep of peace. No worry for him. His experience in the ravine had not changed him. Meanwhile, the limpid shine of the wheeling stars, the night winds, had the mountain all to themselves.

Exhausted after a restless night, afraid of what might be ahead, Melanie took little pleasure in Maximin's gay greeting as they met before seven o'clock on Sunday morning, ready for the trip of less than a mile to La-Salette. Two urchins like us, she thought, going to the priest's house at this hour and demanding to talk to him. If we get in at all, we'll be quickly thrown out. Nor was she pleased when, echoing Grandmother Pra, she said that the lady was the Blessed Virgin, and Maximin simply shrugged.

As they walked past the dew-bright fields and approached the cemetery, they saw the police constable of LaSalette parish coming toward them on the road. "And where are you two going so early in the morning," he demanded in his official voice. Had they asked him where he was going, they might have learned that he was on his way from the house of one town councilor to another's, reminding them of a meeting set for that day. But their part was to answer, not ask. They told him they were headed for the rectory. Uniformed, moustached authority wanted to know why. To tell the priest of what had happened on the mountain yesterday afternoon. And what was that? The story was narrated yet again, while the constable eyed them with professional suspicion. When they had finished, he laughed at them, waved them on their ridiculous errand, but, tramping along on his own errand, he decided it might be well to mention this business to the mayor. Make a report, that was it: "At 6:47 this morning, me being betimes at my duty . . ."

The laughter did little to reassure the timid Melanie as the children came into the rectory yard and, without daring to think that such as they might present themselves at the front of the house, automatically went round to the back. A knock at the kitchen door brought

43

the priest's housekeeper, an inquisitive spinster named Françoise, a woman not unkind but inclined to be high-handed if she could get away with it.

Yes? They wanted to see the priest. See the priest at this hour? He was not to be disturbed. As a matter of fact, he was at his desk, writing his sermon. Evidently not a notably forehanded preacher, this, writing his sermon just before Mass. But they *must* see the priest. Must they, indeed? And why? They had something of great importance to tell him. They could tell it to her; it was the same thing. Seeing that she was immovable, the children began their recital.

Father Perrin, in a nearby room, heard them begin. Distraction this early. As they continued, he laid down his pen. For a while he sat motionless, then moved noiselessly toward the door leading to the kitchen. When the account was complete, he stepped into the kitchen. "I've heard everything you've said, my children, everything." And he began to weep. Tears! Like the lady's. This was still another reaction to their story. Selme's quizzical silence, Grandmother Pra's exultant cry, Pra's shout of anger, the constable's belittling laugh. And now, from the priest, tears. "You are fortunate, my children," he said to them, "for it must have been the Blessed Virgin whom you saw."

"You see, Mémin," Melanie burst out, "I told you that it was the Blessed Virgin."

It was Mass time. Father Perrin must get over to the church, and Maximin must hurry off to meet Selme for the trip home. Melanie, who had so seldom fulfilled the Sunday obligation, decided that she would do so here and now. She slipped into a pew at the back of the church, unnoticed by the strangers who made up the congregation. Mass began. Melanie looked intently at the statue of the Blessed Virgin. Was this the lady?

44

She was still engaged in her scrutiny when Father Perrin mounted the pulpit.

She was astonished, alarmed, at what he began to say. He was telling the people of her and Maximin's experience on the mountain. His voice was choked with emotion. Tears streamed down his face. His hands trembled. His words were unintelligible save by someone who already knew the story. The people peered at one another, mystified. What in the world was he talking about? Shakes of the head, raising of the eyebrows. Melanie understood him, of course. And there was one other who did so, M. Peytard, the mayor.

Peytard had had the story from the constable. He had dismissed it as preposterous. A prank on the part of the children. He was disturbed as the priest continued. Peytard was a responsible man, and highly respected. He had had more schooling than anyone in the parish except the priest. And the priest ought to know better than to blurt this thing from the pulpit directly after hearing it for the first time, without testing it, sifting it. This was decidedly not the way of the Church, so slow, so cautious about approving as authentic any manifestation alleged to be supernatural. Devout and goodhearted this priest surely was, and perhaps his judgment on the children's story was right, but obviously his judgment in hastily announcing it in public was grievously at fault. Maybe the people didn't know at the moment what the preacher was talking about, but they soon would. And then what a ruckus! The mayor was vexed.

Melanie was frightened. Mass finished, she was one of the first out of church, and she ran from the town, eager to get back to Ablandins. But she was to know no peace that day. Ablandins was buzzing, and Peytard was soon on his way there.

45

After Mass the council had met, but the prepared agenda was ignored. One of the councilors was Jean Moussier, from Ablandins, who, the night before, had inevitably heard the story there. Had the councilors caught what Father Perrin was saying, asked the mayor as he called them to order. No. Well, he would tell them, and Moussier would fill out the narrative and describe the excitement in Ablandins, which, remember, was in their territory. What a nuisance! It would have to be put to a stop, at once.

In the afternoon, Peytard stepped out toward Ablandins. He would not advertise his purpose, but would casually drop in at the Pras' house, for a friendly visit. Baptiste Pra welcomed him, offered him a drink. The two men sat at the kitchen table, a bottle of wine between them, while the rest of the household went about their routine. When an offhand atmosphere had been established, Peytard spoke for the first time to Melanie. He would like to hear that story she had been telling. Would she repeat it? She would, and she did, straightforwardly, not in the least flustered. He listened without comment. Then, when she was through, he said, mildly, "Be very careful, my child, not to add anything or suppress anything."

"I have said everything that the beautiful lady told me to say," was her reply. She stood there, in her plain dress, her work-signed hands under her apron, returning his level look.

He smiled, nodded, joked with his host, called out something to Mme. Pra, then shot a piercing question at the child, one intended to trap her in a contradiction. She was not trapped. So it went for some time, Peytard intermixing irrelevancies and jests with sudden remarks or queries directed at the girl and designed to confuse her and induce her to say something at odds with her original story. She did not budge from it. Still smiling, he let a hint of threat come into his voice, his words. She withdrew nothing, altered nothing, nor did she give any sign of perturbation. He gazed at her severely, spoke brusquely, in a menacing tone. If she continued to recount this falsehood, he would quickly have her flung into jail. The child made no answer, stood her ground unruffled.

A change of tactics was indicated. First he alluded solicitously to the jibes for which she would be the target if she went around talking such nonsense. Did she want to be the laughingstock of the countryside, the butt of snickering scorn? She was unmoved. She had her task to perform, cost what it may. Slowly, meaningfully, the mayor thrust his hand into his pocket, withdrew it. Onto the table he flung half-a-dozen five-franc pieces. They rang on the wood, winked in the slanting sunlight. They were hers, on condition that she repeat her story no more and put it out of her mind. Melanie looked at the shining coins. Twenty-five, thirty francs. Three months' wages. A magic surprise for her family when she went back to the hovel in Corps. She looked, but kept her hands under her apron. Peytard scooped up the coins, reached for one of her hands, and clapped the treasure into it. As if they were burning coals, the child of extremest poverty threw them back on the table.

"You could give me this whole house full of crowns," she cried, "and still you would not stop me from saying what I have seen and heard!"

Peytard frowned, swept up the money, pushed back the chair, left the house. He was an educated man. Had he ever read much about Jeanne d'Arc? If so, did he recall any of it as he stalked out of the fruitless interview?

But was it fruitless? Manifestly, the mayor had failed to accomplish his purpose: to quash the incident once and for all, to show up the story as a fantastic invention, to silence the trouble-making children. It would soon be generally known that, try though he might, try what he might, he did not shake Melanie or get her to vary her account by a word or persuade her to say no more of it.

Baptiste Pra sat on at the table, reflecting. A remarkable thing, the way that simple, unlettered, fearful Melanie had withstood all the mayor's tricks, twists, threats, the way she had refused the considerable sum of money. The child was convinced that she spoke the ungarnished truth, and she was consistent in repeating it unchanged. The lengthy interview bore this fruit, that it induced Pra to abandon his attitude of disbelief and hostility. There was something to this thing. It was going to be heard from in the future. Get Melanie's story down on paper—that was the right course. He must talk it over, right away, with Selme and Moussier.

Selme had brought Maximin to Corps and returned to Ablandins. A basket had been packed with butter and cheese, as Giraud had stipulated. And as soon as Maximin got back from LaSalette, Selme told him to fetch the goat and Loulou and they would be on their way to Corps.

When they came into Corps, the congregation for the last Mass was emerging from the church into the mellow autumn day. Selme and Maximin made for the latter's house. Giraud, as might have been expected, was not there. Already he had taken his accustomed place in the drinkshop, in the midst of his rowdy friends, and when Selme finally found him, the wheelwright was well primed with wine. Selme informed him that Maximin had been brought home. Was the boy all right? The boy was fine. And the agreed payment? That had been delivered in Giraud's kitchen. But there was something Selme wanted to say before leaving. Yes? Well, yesterday, when the boy was out of Selme's sight for a while, he and a girl named Melanie Mathieu (she was from Corps, by the way) had met a woman, so they said. The farmer ran through the children's story. As it unfolded, Giraud scowled. His friends hooted. They doubled up with laughter, smote the table, poked Giraud in the ribs, kept up a stream of indelicate, contemptuous comment. Everyone in the café joined in the derisive chorus. Selme was glad to get out of the place, with its bleary windows, its stale air, its coarse, bitter-flavored jollification.

Giraud stayed on, his pride touched on the raw that his son was involved in some pious buffoonery. Now and again he made an angry retort as a burning jest came arrowing at him; sometimes his only response was a racking asthmatic cough. At last, at nine o'clock or so, he got up unsteadily, paid for his drinks, and lurched homeward. He would deal with that clown of a son.

There had been no warm welcome for Maximin from his querulous stepmother. He had not tarried with her after Selme left, but made for his grandmother's. She, at least, would be glad to see him, he knew, and he to see her after a whole week's separation. The old woman embraced him, asked him how he had fared so far from home, and so long, and at such hard work. The talkative boy gave her a lengthy, jumbled answer, but when it came to the happenings of Saturday afternoon, he spoke with unusual coherence, telling the experience fully, clearly. His grandmother's smile disappeared. She watched him closely as he went rapidly through the story. As he finished, tears welled up in her eyes, spilled down her bony face. She knew this child thoroughly. The story was unlike anything she had ever heard from him. Nothing in it jibed with what he had ever said. It was the kind of thing he had never heard of, would never have bothered about. He had not the imagination to invent it, nor were his inclinations such as to induce the least interest in it if someone else had invented it. This was indeed an actual experience, minutely reported. Who the beautiful lady was the old woman could more than surmise. If *she* said things so frightening, other things so consoling, there could be no doubting their fulfillment. And to think that it was to Mémin, scapegrace, motherless, unpromising Mémin, that she had spoken. His grandmother was overcome.

Soon her friends had the news, and all day long they came in relays to her kitchen. Times past counting Maximin had to rehearse the story, to answer the same questions, to listen to the same comments. It got unbearably tiresome, for his one wish had been that, after seeing his grandmother, he might go looking for his friends and zestfully resume those rough-and-tumble games of which he had been deprived for a week. He was yet to learn that his friends would no longer admit him to their clamorous company and pursuits. Impressed by the talk of their elders and the attention soon to come to Maximin, they saw him no longer as the Mémin of old, and made it clear that his place was not with their sort.

Heavy-eyed, his feet dragging, he was escorted home and packed off to bed. He slept. Then he was startled awake as someone seized him and dragged him from the wretched bed. It was his father, back at last from the drinkshop and as full of wrath as he was of wine. The boy was pulled into the kitchen, blinking, still in a stupor. His father flung himself into a chair.

His stepmother, in another chair, stared at Maximin, her eyes glittering with distrust, and yet with wonder, in the lamplight. What was all this insanity attributed to him and sure to mark him as the fool of the world, his father roared.

Must he tell the story yet again? His father shouted a command that he speak. He began. Silence from his stepmother. Snorts from his father, and extravagant gestures of impatience. When he started to repeat the first words of the beautiful lady's discourse, his father jumped up. "Who on earth would be clever enough to be able to teach you so much in an instant, when for years I've been killing myself trying to get you to memorize the 'Our Father' and the 'Hail Mary,' and you still don't know them?" Through the vinous fog a swordlike question had cut its way, a question with shattering implications. These Giraud would not face. He would have no more of the whole affair. To bed! Sleep. Forget.

If the light was extinguished in the Giraud kitchen, the lamp still burned in Pra's kitchen up in Ablandins. Baptiste Pra had summoned Selme and Moussier, as he had planned, and the three men had, in seclusion and with inching care, talked over every detail of the children's story and its aftermath. Melanie, wilted after the wearing day, was on hand for them to question. As the evening waned, his two neighbors came to share Pra's certainty that the girl was telling something objectively true, completely factual, and, further, that the beautiful lady was the Blessed Virgin.

Pra got out several sheets of paper, a pen, some ink. These were seldom used, even seen, in this house, for countryfolk only rarely had need for them. Pra grasped the rusted pen, dipped it in the pewter pot with its crust of dried ink, set himself to the sweaty labor of writing. Once more Melanie started on the story, but now very slowly, so that Pra, bent close to the paper, might get every word right. His script was misshapen, his spelling not without its pathetic errors, but how right was his instinct in giving documentary form, as quickly as possible, to what the unforgettable voice had said on the mountain just the day before. Line after wavering line was set down as the lamp yellowed the four earnest faces, line after wavering line forming a stout net to catch and hold a wonder that would dazzle the world.

Monday morning Giraud awoke to the shrieking of his younger children. They were crying for breakfast, quarreling over their few, seedy playthings, answering their mother back as she reproved them. The previous day's drinking made itself felt in Giraud's queasy stomach, ballooning head. More noise. Someone was at the door, hammering to be heard above the din. Mme. Giraud scurried to see who it was. A man who introduced himself as Peytard, the mayor of LaSalette. The fuss and shame of the day before, until then forgotten, rushed back into Giraud's mind. And now more trouble. What did M. Peytard want? Wasn't this where Maximin Giraud lived, the boy who for the past week had been working for Selme up on the mountain? Yes. Peytard wished to have a few words with him. Maximin was roused, summoned. Peytard wanted to speak to him alone. When he was allowed to do so, he wasted neither time nor ceremony. "You miserable boy," he said, in an angry voice, "what have you done? You've spread abroad a story which has upset everyone and can only lead to trouble. I wouldn't want to be in your shoes; in fact, I'd consider myself better off if I had killed someone than if I'd made up the yarn you did, along with Melanie."

The abrupt, heavy frontal attack did not faze Maximin. He insisted that he and Melanie had made up nothing, had told just what they had seen and heard. The mayor made more explicit threats: the police would pounce on Maximin, the judge before whom he would cower would condemn him, and then off to prison with him. Still the boy did not falter. He was speaking the exact truth. The exasperated Peytard realized that, no more than with Melanie, would he have any success with this child. He warned Maximin to listen carefully to what he was going to say. Next Sunday he was to come to LaSalette and go with the mayor and Melanie to the mountain where this meeting with a woman was supposed to have taken place. There, on the spot, the infant myth would be disposed of. But Maximin would be only too glad to return to the scene of the happiest moments of his eleven years.

4

At least one person in Corps held aloof from the commotion which rocked the town during the ensuing week. Every day saw a repetition, an aggrandizement, of the doings of the Sunday of Maximin's return. The curious besieged Giraud's house, to the wheelwright's fury. He tongue-lashed his son, but to no avail. If Maximin stepped into the street, he was waylaid, importuned to tell his story. People of such quality as Corps could boast and who had never before taken note of the lad with the unsightly dog jogging along after him now tried to lure him to their homes. A frequently used stratagem was to have someone invite Giraud to the café and buy him drink after drink; meanwhile, Maximin would be taken to a house where there was room for a sizable audience, then started on his story and plied with questions. Everyone had a go at interrogating him: the doctor, for example, and the notary. Even the most trenchant or subtle of them could not rattle or trip him. Belief in the truth of his story began to prevail. The tide of excitement rose in the town. But in the midst of it was one island of calm reserve, the rectory.

The parish priest of Corps was Father Mélin, a man younger than Father Jacques Perrin of LaSalette. He had been an assistant at the Cathedral in Grenoble and knew the bishop very well. The latter had shown particular confidence in him by appointing him not only pastor of St. Peter's in Corps, but also archpriest of that section of the diocese. This position gave him a certain amount of special jurisdiction as the bishop's local representative. Father Perrin, in showing the children out of the LaSalette rectory on Sunday morning, had told Maximin to go to Father Mélin as soon as he got to Corps. Maximin forgot, or in any case failed, to do so. And during the week he gave no thought to his pastor.

But his pastor, despite the silence he maintained, was evidently giving much thought to Maximin and the whole affair which was agitating the town. He kept informed of every development. Thus, on Saturday, September 26, he knew that Melanie was in Corps to visit her family, that her father had given her a reception anything but gentle and had been at least as fierce as Giraud in attacking the story as a fiction and the teller of the story as a faker who deserved to be thrashed. Father Mélin decided to act. On that Saturday he sent for the girl and the boy.

They had never before approached this house where the priest with alert eyes, firm wide mouth, and craggy chin now gravely received them. From him no ready tears, as from Father Perrin; no deference such as was already being shown them by some of their fellow townsmen; on the other hand, no insinuating smirk, either. He treated them in the strictly correct way: as two children of his flock from whom he had every right to get an explanation of what they had been saying in a matter touching religion.

He put Melanie in the kitchen, took Maximin into the parlor. There he asked the boy to tell his story. As Father Mélin listened, his face was inscrutable. When Maximin had finished, the priest asked, "Is that all?" "No," said Maximin, "there is something else, but the Blessed Virgin forbade me to repeat it." Maximin was now calling the beautiful lady the Blessed Virgin, as he had heard Grandmother Pra and Father Perrin do. Father Mélin made no comment on this or on anything else. He got up, called Melanie in from the kitchen, directed Maximin to step out, and then heard the girl's account of the happening. Again, "Is that all?" Again, a reference to a secret. Again, no attempt to pry. Next the priest brought the children together and cross-examined them, asking question after probing question.

Whatever conclusion he reached he kept strictly to himself. He gave no indication of his mind as he sent the girl and boy away. But this was not to be the end of his inquiry, for he told them that on the following Monday, September 28, he would go to LaSalette and expected them to accompany him.

But tomorrow they were to visit the mountain with the mayor. Two trips on two successive days? And arduous trips, too, at least for Maximin, who would have to cover the distance from Corps four times. It seems not to have occurred to them to object, to suggest that the expeditions be merged. They wordlessly accepted their pastor's mandate.

Just as docilely they presented themselves to M. Peytard on Sunday, the 27th, as he had ordered. The mayor still hoped that a show of force might get them to retract. He brought along the sergeant of police in Corps. They were not impressed. Rather, they were seized with delight at being again in the place of the apparition. They ran to the ravine, pointed to the rock at the dried-up spring, and said it was here that they had first noticed the light, here that, a minute later, they had discerned the woman seated. They re-enacted the event, describing what they had seen, what they had felt; giving in full what had been said to them (all but the secrets), what they had said; following the course of the beautiful lady's steps—from the rock, across the stream, then up the ravine, to the rise at its end. They showed where, at each point, they had stood, and what they had done.

All this they did spontaneously, with relish, without any sign of embarrassment, constraint. Here was no minutely contrived, warily executed performance by actors nervous lest they deviate from an effortfully learned script. The children, Peytard grudgingly recognized, were unforcedly and without hesitation or strain reliving an actuality which was graphic and precise in their memory.

But he still thought with distaste of the rumpus in Ablandins, LaSalette, Corps, and perhaps of the government's displeasure when the news reached Grenoble and even Paris, as it surely would if a halt could not be called. The sergeant of police now intervened, heavy-handedly. "You're lying," he roared at Maximin. From his pocket he took a piece of rope. "I am going to tie your hands and take you off to prison." The boy cringed. This was at a time, when, to a child, a policeman was olympian and well nigh omnipotent, not a friend to be hailed familiarly or with taunts. But Maximin quickly realized what must be his reply.

"All your threats will not make me say anything different from what we saw and heard."

"Well, then, tell me where this woman went to."

"She disappeared into the light, and the light prevented us from seeing where she went."

"And you did not see her after that?"

"No. She didn't return to tell us where she'd gone."

"Well, she's been found. Some soldiers have seized her and put her in prison."

"Clever indeed, the person who could seize her!"

The sergeant, so neatly scored off, looked at Peytard, who gave him a slight, wintry smile. Nothing would prise these two from their story; methods shrewd or crass were equally useless. The most telling thing was their conduct here on the mountain. The mayor gazed long, wonderingly, respectfully at the ravine.

Father Mélin found his journey of the next day extremely taxing. It took him four hours to get to the mountain. This was not a place easy to reach. No one would choose it as the goal of an easy jaunt, a holiday excursion. One had to pay, in pain and sweat, for a visit to this height. He brought his sacristan along, and four others who could be relied on to prove keen observers. The occasion was not to be one for sentimentality, but for cold, dry-eyed scrutiny of the scene and the children who persisted in giving it an aura of glory.

As yesterday for the mayor, so today for their pastor, Melanie and Maximin reconstructed the event from beginning to end. Here they had eaten their lunch, here they had lain down to sleep, this was how Melanie had started up, this was where they found the cows grazing, this was the manner of their discovery of the light. So it went, every word, every gesture critically watched by the priest and his little company.

Father Mélin was profoundly affected. The authenticity of the story was, each moment, clearer. How easily the children moved through it, how natural was the flow of speech, action. Neither contradicted the other, and this latest recounting was in entire accord with those previously given. Poor, ignorant, far from pious little ones, they were privileged beyond their imagining. But he said nothing of this, and his emotion he completely concealed. Instead, cool in manner, he shot questions at the pair, and so did the five other adults. The crossfire of interrogation and objection made no dent on the astonishing narrative.

Someone suggested that, before leaving, they say some prayers. Father Mélin saw nothing amiss in this. They knelt in the ravine, the first of incalculably many who would do so. The priest took out his rosary, and began the recitation: "I believe . . ." The "Hail Mary's" followed one another, as numerous as the roses on the beautiful lady's costume. The litany of our Lady was said: "Virgin most powerful. Virgin most merciful . . . Cause of our joy . . . Refuge of sinners. Comforter of the afflicted. Help of Christians." The lovely, heartening titles took wing in the crisping air.

It was time to leave. One of the men went to the rock by the dried-out spring, meaning to knock off a piece to bring home with him. Father Mélin, seeing what was being attempted, said that the rock, on which the beautiful lady had sat, should not be broken. Rather, they would carry the whole thing down to Corps. And what about this spring's being dried out, and giving water only after heavy rains or when the snow higher up on the mountains was melting? Now the spring was abundantly gushing water, in a steady stream. This was something new, unaccountable. Using a wine bottle emptied during the party's lunch, the priest secured some of the water.

The downward journey gave him plenty of time to think over the occurrences of the last week. As he was to say later, he left the mountain convinced that the Queen of Heaven had, in simple yet astounding fact, appeared to Melanie and Maximin and had spoken what they steadfastly reported. But he must not betray his own view. Bishop Philibert de Bruillard had to be informed. Father Mélin would compose a letter at leisure, and put it in the post for Grenoble. It was up to the bishop to determine what, if anything, would be done about the apparition. Knowing the bishop as he did, Father Mélin could foresee two things.

In the first place, his superior would be irreproachably prudent. He was a sensibly cautious man, neither precipitate nor indecisive. Moreover, he was an expert in, and a stickler for, proper canonical procedure. It would not sit well with him that Father Jacques Perrin, at LaSalette, had preached about the apparition less than twenty-four hours after it took place. That was not the Church's way, nor was it Bishop de Bruillard's, and it might go hard with the well-meaning, but regrettably injudicious, shepherd of the mountain hamlets that he had spoken openly and approvingly of an untried wonder. No, the bishop would permit no syllable of official recognition for a long time yet. Whether there would ever be any official recognition, or whether public condemnation would be pronounced, would depend on the findings of a close, disinterested, extended investigation.

But in the second place, Father Mélin could predict that Bishop de Bruillard would not wave the matter away as absurd and not to be dwelt upon for even a second. The bishop was a man of sterling faith, notable piety. He had that wisdom which is an acute awareness of the ways of providence, ways that to the mediocre, half-blinded by trivialities, seen at variance with reason. The story would immediately interest the bishop. He would seriously study it and be ready to credit it should its genuineness be soundly established.

Father Mélin could, then, face the future equably. He wished, and even as he walked along began to pray, for some sign from our Lady that she had actually appeared to the children. A miracle, for example, obviously linked with the scene of the apparition, which would set the seal of heavenly approval on their story. For himself, he required no such supporting witness. The children were telling the truth, and when you analyzed what they had to say, every sentence of it was translucent with verisimilitude, startling congruity, and meaning.

How like our Lady, to be solicitous for her people. That trait of hers leaped from the pages of the Gospel. Hardly had she the tremendous news that in her womb the Son of God would take on a human nature, than she was off for the hill town of Karem in remote Judea, to visit her aged cousin Elizabeth, miraculously with child. She took to the southward road, to walk it for many a mile, that she might be with Elizabeth and do for her whatever was needful. So she began in her role as Mother of the divine Saviour; so had she always continued. It was, then, wholly in character for her to show her concern for mankind, to exert prodigious effort to avert the divine displeasure from those who were defying God and breaking His commandments. Were they not her children, and does not the motherly heart try to ward off punishment however condign?

Father Mélin knew, to his sorrow, how well-justified were the reproaches uttered on the mountain. On the basis of his own observation he could frame a jeremiad. There was an ever more common ignoring of God, a refusal, hardening into habit, to render Him honor, to give Him even the crumbs of His due. In Corps and its environs, as well as in the rest of France and the rest of the world, God was increasingly disregarded. Sunday, for example, was no longer reserved and sacred to Him, as He had long since appointed it should be. A straggling few came to Mass; but most lay late abed, or worked as on Monday or Thursday, or gave themselves over to drinking or dancing or gaming. It was worst of all in the fine days of summer, when the congregation comprised chiefly women of late middle age and beyond. When winter grimly set in, others came, but out of boredom or a desire to get some sport from disrespectful comment on the ceremonies and the sermon. It was as if they were dead to religion, no longer quick to spiritual reality.

Cursing and swearing were the accustomed punctuation of ordinary speech. In anger, in jest, in protestation, in emphasis, God's name was automatically used, sometimes in a way nothing less than horrible. Used thus, it was ever more seldom used in prayer. Where piety had once blossomed there were now but a few blanched and wilted stalks. The Angelus bell was no more than a reminder of the hour of day, not a reminder to lift up mind and heart to the eternal. Once, the penitential season of Lent had been scrupulously observed; the countryfolk had been noted for their austerity during the forty days from Ash Wednesday to Easter. But now the sense of sin was like a severed or withered nerve, and the necessity of mortification was consequently unrecognized.

The children could never have drawn an indictment so comprehensive, detailed, apposite. They had grown up to take the present state of affairs as normal; they had no criteria for perceiving wherein it was monstrous. To be oblivious of God, to treat Sunday as in no wise exceptional, to go never or but rarely to Mass, to be profane and blasphemous in speech, to consider Lent as nothing different from the rest of the year—this was what everyone did, what they observed all about them, what they did themselves. They had no religious training; not one of the commandments could they recite. How, then, could they concoct this set of acute criticisms?

Then there were the warnings, so specific, so pertinent. The crops would fail. Hunger would be general, and after it something more bitter and lethal: famine. Children would fall sick, agonize, die, their parents powerless to stay the ravages of strange disease. But this constantly accelerating course of calamity would be checked, reversed, if the people abandoned their godlessness and turned again to their Father and to conduct becoming His children. How all this conformed to the pattern traced and retraced in the pages of the Bible. It was something quite beyond the comprehension of a boy and girl illiterate, especially so where religion was concerned. Unthinkable that they could have originated this cry for penance, for ploughing up the iron-hard earth, harrowing, pulverizing it, so that the good seed might find lodging, and rain and sun whereon to work.

Father Mélin could smile under his broad-brimmed hat when he recalled the expression on Maximin's face as he told of the beautiful lady's knowledge of the incident of a year ago on the roadside near Coin. The lad was still astonished every time he came to this part of the story. She knew what the farmer had said, what his father had said, what the three of them had done. She could repeat, to the letter, the conversation between himself and his father when they were alone on the road.

Now, thinking of Maximin, he looked at the boy. There would be those who would reject the apparition after one glance at him. There would be those whose attitude would be: "What! The Blessed Virgin appear to this pair? Don't be silly. It wouldn't be seemly. Only size them up, consider who and what they are, and you will see the absurdity of it. If the Blessed Virgin was going to appear to anyone, it would be to someone respectable, someone in a position to help her, or to a person very holy, probably a nun praying day and night in chapel and cell, like that Catherine Labouré in Paris. Show a little sense, a little reverence! Here you have a pair of ragamuffins who, by their own admission, pray hardly ever, infrequently darken the door of a church. Why, we know that the boy, when taken to church against his will a few times, sneaked out before Mass was well begun. They know nothing about religion, these two, and care less. Thoroughly miserable specimens both, the very dregs. And you can suggest that the Blessed Virgin would so demean herself as to associate with the likes of them? The very idea that she could give them a message for the world is preposterous."

How little they knew the Gospels, these worthy people. Wouldn't they be incensed, apoplectic, were you to tell them that they sounded just like the Pharisees? The Pharisees were sure that the Nazarene could not be the Messias because he associated with the riff-raff, entered their houses, ate and drank with them, spoke kindly to them, showed solicitude for them. He was surrounded with raw, untutored fishermen, figures of fun from the despicable hinterland, and had the effrontery to commission them to go about lecturing their betters on God, God's wishes, God's ways. Scandalous! Ridiculous on the face of it! No, the Messias would have the good judgment to come to the people of substance and decency, and use them as conveyors of whatever word he would have announced to the unregenerate

65

crowd. Curious victory of the long dead Pharisees, that they had so many imitators, so many who thought and spoke as they did, so many centuries later. The Blessed Virgin a stuffy *bourgeoise*—here was pharisaism with a vengeance.

It was one of the most arresting and conclusive aspects of this affair that the apparition should be to such as Maximin and Melanie. The Blessed Virgin had freely associated with those among whom her Son moved familiarly, regardless of what the Pharisees might think. His ways were hers. When He saw need of instruction, excitation, He went directly to those in need of them, to the people. How typical were Maximin and Melanie of their times, their surroundings. You might have finecombed France for years and not come up with two who so exactly and eloquently represented the end product of irreligion. Miserable duo, pitifully neglected, strangers to the animating warmth of love, early indentured to toil, their souls desertlike in barrenness of knowledge of their Father and their destiny, unacquainted with the graces, lights, consolations which follow upon such knowledge, existing, subsisting, but hardly living, with nothing to look forward to save a hard, even harsh, lot and then the voracious, annihilating dust. They were the speaking image, the incarnation of the woe of the world. Truly, they were the lost sheep whom the heavenly Shepherdess would walk the lonely mountain reaches to find.

But wait a minute. If you could get the self-righteous to see that, they would voice yet another objection, and with the feline smugness of a lawyer propounding what he knows to be the unanswerable question. Why should the Blessed Virgin appear to children? Wouldn't it be far more logical for her to come to an adult, a person in the plenitude of his powers, mature, discriminating, balanced, instant in understanding? But this was not the unanswerable question at all.

Father Mélin could, from experience, contrast the attitudes of children and adults, perhaps the very same persons as children and as adults. How trusting they were in the first years, how open-minded, how simple, how candid. Life had not yet warped and soured them, had not yet pickled them in the brine of mistrust, had not yet complicated them or indurated them or imprisoned them in the bonds of their own conceit. You can speak to a child where you cannot speak to an adult. You can communicate to a child what you cannot communicate to an adult. The child will not denature what you say; but by the time an adult has run it through all the filters with which he has cluttered his consciousness over the years, it will be unrecognizable. Why had our Lord held up little children as models? Because what you say to them they will take literally. They will not discount it, adapt it, interpret it away.

Yet, if children were to be chosen as channels for a message to the world, why not precocious children instead of this backward boy and girl. What does "precocious" mean? In its native sense, it means ripened or cooked before the usual time. In a child, it means to have some adult traits before adulthood. No, these two represented perfectly that springtime simplicity of childhood which was required. You realized that as you observed them going through their story time after time. There were no additions, no glosses. They did not attempt to construe or apply what it was they said. They simply repeated, with unswerving fidelity, what they saw, what they heard. They were ideal to the purpose.

But here they were back in Corps. Melanie they had

left in the hamlet of Ablandins, that cluster of thatched stone houses, seemingly as sturdy as the mountains, where she still had some weeks of her service to complete. The foot-sore company broke up.

While still on the mountain Father Mélin had decided to bring some of the water from the mysteriously active spring to one of his parishioners who had for some time been seriously ill. This was one Mme. Anglot. Everyone knew of her illness, its persistence despite every remedy. One of her neighbors saw the bottle being brought to the rectory by a member of the party which had accompanied Father Mélin. "What have you in that bottle," she asked.

"Some water from LaSalette."

"Who's it for?"

"For the priest."

The woman told Mme. Anglot. Within fifteen minutes, the same neighbor was at the rectory, glass in hand, asking to see Father Mélin. "I've come," she told him, "on behalf of Mme. Anglot, to ask for some of that water from LaSalette. She thinks that it would help her."

The priest was surprised that anyone should attribute special virtue to water from LaSalette, surprised, too, that his intention had been anticipated. He had made up his mind to bring a portion of the water to Mme. Anglot, but, before he could get round to doing so, here was someone seeking it for her. He filled the glass. "Look," he said, smiling, "you tell Mme. Anglot that we shall all scold the Blessed Virgin if she doesn't cure our good friend."

Mme. Anglot began a novena to our Lady. At its outset she was painfully sick. She could retain no food, and was wasting away for lack of nourishment. Each day of the novena she drank a few drops of the water

68

from LaSalette, and with these she had no difficulty. On the ninth day, as Father Mélin himself could testify, she got out of bed, walked about without weakness, went to the table and ate heartily. Her family, having seen her so debilitated and distressed, could not believe their eyes. But there it was; she had regained her health.

The fact had to be admitted, and Father Mélin did so, but he took care to call it something extraordinary, no more. He said nothing of a miracle. It was not yet time for such talk.

But it was time for him to write to the bishop. Early in October he set down the story as fully as possible. "The report of these two children," he wrote, "has had an enormous impact hereabouts, even on the men. I questioned them separately, both here in the rectory and on the mountain, which I reached only after four hours of punishing travel. The public functionaries made threats with a view to silencing them, and money was offered to induce them to say something different from what they had been telling. Neither threats nor promises availed in getting them to change their story. They always say the very same thing and to whoever wants to listen to them. I have gone very deliberately into every bit of information which I was able to lay hands on. I have found nothing which suggests in the remotest way either trickery or lying . . .

"There are several other circumstances and certain facts pertaining to this apparition, but I haven't space to mention them all here. I submit these details to the bishop, who will give what orders he thinks best. It is the view of the people, naturally, that the Mother of God has come to warn the world before her Son rains down punishments. My own conviction, in the light of all the evidence I have been able to gather, is identical with the people's, and I believe that this warning is a great favor from heaven. I have no need of further wonders, to believe. But my intense desire would be that God, in His mercy, should work some new marvel to confirm the first."

A few days later, Bishop de Bruillard sent the following letter to each priest of his diocese:

"Doubtless you know of the extraordinary events which are said to have taken place in the parish of LaSalette, near Corps.

"I urge you to consult the Synodal Statutes which I gave my diocese in 1829. Here is what will be found on page 94:

" 'We forbid, under pain of suspension incurred *ipso facto,* the announcement, printing, or publishing of anything about any new miracle, no matter what pretext of notoriety there may be, unless it have the approval of the Holy See or our own, after an examination which can only be exact and rigid.'

"We have in no way pronounced on the events in question. Wisdom and duty require of you, therefore, the greatest reserve and, above all, a complete silence on this subject in the pulpit.

"Nevertheless, someone has taken the liberty of putting out a lithographed picture, with some verses attached to it.

"I tell you, Father, that this publication not only has not been approved by me, but has caused me extreme annoyance, and I have formally and severely condemned it. Therefore, be on your guard and give an example of prudent reserve which you will not fail to recommend to others."

Father Mélin had correctly judged what the bishop's attitude would be. Father Jacques Perrin's transfer from the parish of LaSalette was announced. He was succeeded by a priest with the same surname, but not the same inclination to premature utterance, Father Louis Perrin.

5

Letters from Corps, from LaSalette, from other parts of his diocese, from beyond his diocese began to pour in on Bishop de Bruillard. Father Mélin was writing to him almost every day from Corps. Father Louis Perrin was making frequent reports from LaSalette. Other priests of the area were sending him their views. Lay folk were telling him what they thought, what he should do, what he shouldn't do. Some of the letters were weighted with official seals. It was an inky deluge. But it would take more than this to disconcert the doughty churchman of eighty-one who ruled the diocese of Grenoble.

Philibert de Bruillard was a native of Dijon. He was ordained, at the age of twenty-four, in the year that saw the loosing of the Revolution. His first assignment was as a teacher of philosophy and theology at the celebrated seminary of St. Sulpice in Paris. While the Terror raged in the capital, the young priest remained there, secretly performing the sacred functions, ministering to all he could reach in the turmoil and horror whirling like an undiminishing hurricane through the passion-darkened city of light.

He later undertook parish work, serving as an assistant at the church of St. Sulpice, and then as pastor of the churches of St. Nicolas du Chardonnet and St. Etienne du Mont. Professor, assistant, pastor, in turbulent times, when the thunder and lightning of violence shook the city, and fear was like a palpable fog, in the years of imperial glory which brought the Church further problems, in the years of defeat and abasement which meant still further difficulties. Besides, he had been spiritual director of St. Madeleine Sophie Barat, foundress of the Religious of the Sacred Heart, before she entered religion. He had weathered unexampled strife; he had had a part in the formation of a saint. And now for twenty-five years he had wisely and temperately ordered the diocese of Grenoble.

The excitement over the apparition would not perturb him. He would not grow panicky in the swelling aftermath of the purported event and hastily condemn it. Nor would he be carried away into imprudent approbation. He would proceed composedly, intelligently.

He read with acute interest the account of the lady in tears, who spoke of her efforts to stay her son's vengeance, who said that, whatever they did by way of prayer and penance, men could never equal what she had endured for them. Expert in theology as this former professor of the subject was, steeped in mystical and ascetical doctrine as this spiritual director of a saint was, he would not conclude, as had some unread or ill-read in theology, that such features of the supposed apparition were enough in themselves to prove the lady could not be the Blessed Virgin. Not in the least. If anything, these features bore down heavily in the other scale.

For the Blessed Virgin was Co-Redemptrix. To Christ's Passion she had joined her own compassion.

Passion and compassion were each on a different level, each of a different character and worth, just as those enduring them differed: Christ being divine as well as human; His Mother being, though the fairest and most privileged of creatures, human and no more. But her suffering had been for men, for the sinful race; it had been meritorious; it had been efficacious. And it was precisely on Calvary, as His Passion and her compassion came each to its exquisite climax, that her Son had given her to all humanity as its Mother. She was to be to all men, in every generation, their Mother, as she was His Mother. A spiritual relationship was thus established. She was invested with universal maternal responsibility and authority. She was to have all mortals in her care and sempiternally to intercede for them; and through her would come to them God's graces.

This had been taught by some of the greatest of the doctors of the Church. Scholars were familiar with it, but how many of the people had mastered its intricacies? The children of LaSalette who, according to the reports now piling up on the bishop's desk, were uninformed about more than the first elements of religion, who could only parrot its ABC's, certainly had never heard of such recondite doctrine. And even had they heard of it, they would have comprehended none of it. It was inconceivable that they could have made up what they reported. Their artless recitation of words which they said were spoken to them by a lady emerging from a globe of light, expressed, in homely terms but with exactitude, the loftiest theology.

Some would, in all likelihood, be put off by the homely terms, without distilling the meaning. Some would say, "The Blessed Virgin weeping, talking of the heaviness of her Son's arm and of the pangs she endured for mankind? But she is in heaven, where all is bliss. She enjoys, in a degree above every other human being, the beatific vision. She cannot be sad and cry and suffer." Of course, she cannot. Nor would anything in the description of the alleged apparition suggest that she does. The details which some would find objectionable might well be merely a means of dramatizing for, and putting within the grasp of, beings of sense and imagination the great truths of Mary's compassion, motherly solicitude, powerful intercession.

This matter would have to be looked into. There was no doubt of that. He would personally consider all the letters and have them filed. But he would do more. He would send to LaSalette some of his most astute and level-headed diocesan officials from Grenoble.

Thus, in mid-October, he dispatched to the place of the apparition Father Chambon, superior of the minor seminary, and with him three members of the seminary faculty. They were to investigate painstakingly and to supply him with a written report. The report was completed and in the bishop's hands by November 10. As the file began to bulge, the bishop appointed two commissions to sift it, letter by letter, report by report, and to assay its contents. The commissions were to operate independently of each other, without any exchange of impressions and opinions, and each was to give him its own evaluation and recommendations. One group comprised eight canons of the cathedral; the other, six professors of the Grenoble major seminary. They went to work.

In the meantime, there were new developments daily in Corps and at the scene of the children's encounter with mystery.

The silence advisedly imposed on the clergy for the time being had no effect on the people. Already they were beginning to speak unstudiedly of the Mountain of Our Lady, the Mountain of Our Good Mother, and to it they made pilgrimage singly and in groups. The primitive road through LaSalette and Ablandins had never been so traveled as now. People from Corps, people from beyond Corps, kept coming and asking directions so that one could not for long work uninterruptedly in kitchen or field. The fact that the trip was exhausting, and in its last stages perilous for those not used to the mountains, was no deterrent. And everyone wanted to see Melanie and Maximin. Many offered the children money. It was always declined.

Maximin's stepmother was among these early visitors to the scene of the apparition. Giraud had somewhat relaxed his original attitude. For days he had moodily persisted in his refusal to listen to Maximin's story. Then he chanced to overhear the boy telling it to someone else. When Giraud attempted to intervene, his son said, "The lady spoke of you, too."

This intrigued the wheelwright. "Of me? What did she say?"

Maximin repeated for him that part of the lady's words dealing with the episode beginning near Coin and ending near Corps. True enough, thought Giraud. All that had slipped his mind, but now, recalling it, he found that the event and a stranger's description of it tallied. He was upset. He did not forthwith announce that he was convinced of the truth of the whole story of the apparition, but he no longer forbade Maximin to retail it, and when his wife told him that the boy's grandmother was going up to the mountain, and nervously suggested that she would like to make the trip with the old woman, he did not shout the expected objection. Instead, he readily agreed to her going and urged her to look the place over with all deliberation, to see whether some impostor might not have duped the children.

Mme. Giraud did as directed. Not a sign of a bush, not a sign of a formation of rock or earth behind which a trickster might have hidden. All was bare and open here, so that anyone coming or going could not escape immediate detection. And everything about the place corresponded entirely, minutely, with the children's story. Indeed, there was an atmosphere which spoke to one, compelled one to believe. Giraud heard her out. He was much more affected than he wanted to show, remembering with chagrin his hasty denials, his rages. But his wife could sense the change in him. Wouldn't he himself go up there? It might mean relief from the asthma which chronically plagued him. He growled noncommittally.

But he went, in his own time. He went and was wholly won over. He declared that his asthma was cured; it bothered him no more. Much more important, he returned to the practice of his religion. He went regularly to church, to the sacraments. Indeed, he assisted at daily Mass, with few exceptions, for the rest of his life. He left off his swilling of wine, the strident sessions in the drinkshop, the neglect of his family. He strove to repress his temper, to be all that so long he had not been.

He was not the only one to reform. The lady of the apparition had called on the people to mend their ways. She had served notice that disaster would be the consequence of failure to do so. Her words had not been general or vague. She had mentioned the very abuses which were common in the region; she had specified punishments of which the people knew only too well. But was it the threats alone or chiefly which moved them? May not the tears have been the principal factor? There was something calculated to penetrate the stoniest heart, to awaken the most sluggish soul, in the weeping of one whom they ever more firmly believed to be the Blessed Virgin. A mother may complain, reprove, threaten, and still have little or no effect on an erring son or daughter. But if she weeps, if her love, anxiety, distress pour out in tears, the effect is almost certain. In most cases, the son or daughter will yield, realizing that such devotion and solicitude cannot be trampled on, such anguish cannot be disregarded. The Blessed Virgin in tears because of them! How sharply this brought home to them that they were not the orphans under a blind, impenetrable sky which they had thought themselves; that they were watched over, yearned after; that what they did or didn't do was a cause of intimate concern for someone of magnitude, someone who was the mother par excellence.

M. Mélin, closely observing his people, happily noted the improvement. Sunday ceased to be a day of work. Carousing tapered off. People who had not come to Mass for years were now present Sunday after Sunday. The number of confessions increased; those at Communion were counted in the hundreds. Human respect, which had prevented many from showing themselves Christian, was swept aside. There were certain holidays which had, in the distant past, been of a religious nature, but, in the recent past, had lost all religious significance for the people and degenerated into occasions for drunkenness, pagan revelry, wild dancing. These now resumed their original character. Nor was all this true only of Corps. The priests of the nearby towns saw the same change come over their parishioners. They thought of the words of the Gospel: "An evil tree cannot bring forth good fruit." Here was good fruit in plenty, and the tree from which it came was easily identified.

On November 17, the first formally organized pilgrimage from Corps took place. M. Mélin had nothing to do with getting it up, nor did he take part in it, although he was invited to do so. Among his parishioners was one who longed to go, but could not. This was Mme. Marie Laurent, wife of the town baker. A woman of forty-eight, she had been paralyzed with rheumatism for seven or eight years. She could hobble about a little on crutches, but the effort was excruciatingly painful. Mostly, she sat in a chair during the day, in the doorway if the sun shone. At night she had to be carried to bed, and in the morning lifted out of bed. She could not get to church, and had to content herself with praying at home in the slow hours of idleness or tormenting wakefulness. She asked the pilgrims to remember her when they reached the mountain, and they promised that they would.

They moved off in ordered ranks, no fewer than 600 of them. If, two months earlier, someone had said that in the near future 600 people of the town would make a pilgrimage of four or five hours afoot to the mountains, just as winter was closing in, he would have been considered mad. But here they were, solemnly setting out, praying in unison, singing hymns. And so they continued for the whole exacting journey until, at length, they reached the scene of the apparition, that scene of overwhelming grandeur, with its rugged, cloud-veiled peaks, its sweeping reaches, its pristine air. They gathered in and about the ravine, knelt upon the ground, prayed feelingly, the chorus of adoration and thanksgiving and contrition and petition rebounding from mountain to mountain. The pledge to Mme. Laurent was not forgotten, as they cried full-throatedly upon God. Nothing like this had ever broken upon the seclusion and hush of this place where heaven seemed within reaching distance.

When they had drunk from the once dried-up spring which now emitted water in a flow as steady as that of the lady's tears, they reformed their ranks and started back to Corps. Twilight, then darkness, enfolded them; they continued at their pilgrim's pace, praying. Their singing alerted Corps to their arrival. At every door, spilling lamplight, their number was swelled, as people who had been unable to make the trip now accompanied them to the church, before which the group would disperse. The hymns resounded in the narrow streets.

When the marchers got to the Laurents' house, Mme. Laurent walked out, without her crutches. The crowd was electrified. How was this? What had happened?

As she took a place in the procession, Mme. Laurent explained to those nearest her, and the word was passed back. That afternoon she had taken some water from LaSalette, as she had on every day of the novena she was making. She had felt impelled to get up and walk. She tried it. She could do it. She ran to tell her husband. Then she ran to the church. Ran, after all the years during which she could not get near the church, crippled as she was. But just when had this happened? She fixed the time. It was the very hour when, on the mountain, they had called upon heaven, its Lord, its Queen, to help her. Now, in the cobblestone square in front of the church, the pilgrims gave deafening voice to the *Magnificat*, the canticle spoken by our Lady when she came to Elizabeth's house to give her cousin what help she could.

*"My soul magnifies the Lord, and my spirit rejoices in
God my Saviour;*
*Because He has regarded the lowliness of His hand-
maid; for, behold, henceforth all generations shall call
me blessed;*
*Because He who is mighty has done great things for
me and holy is His name."*

Mme. Laurent had no further need of crutches. The
hard swellings which the rheumatism had caused in her
joints remained, but only as evidence that this woman
had once been severely afflicted with the ailment. The
fact that she could walk without difficulty was evidence that the ailment's grip had been broken. The
local physician, Dr. Calvat, proved to his satisfaction
that this was so. The following Saturday Mme. Laurent
went to church for confession; the following Sunday
she went there for Mass; and when she walked up to
Communion there was craning of necks, along with
whispered exclamations, through the congregation.

News of this undoubtedly had much to do with the
size of the second pilgrimage, held on November 28.
This was to be in thanksgiving for the favor done Mme.
Laurent. More than a thousand (some put the number
at 1,500) gathered to take part in it, among them people from the surrounding countryside and other towns.
All ages were represented, from fresh-faced children
to old people hard put to keep up with their juniors.
The weather did not hold them back. It had turned
bitingly cold, and snow was steadily falling. No matter,
the pilgrimage advanced, headed by the members of
the Corps police force. Along the way, more people fell
in with the group, some of them never known to have
done anything religious before this. Once again there
were the prayers, the hymns; once again, the sound of

supplication surged upon the heights. On this occasion, too, something remarkable was reported. A woman from Dévoluy, suffering from dropsy, had been carried up the mountain by her husband and her son. She declared herself cured after drinking of the water from the spring.

So it went. A third large pilgrimage took place, and the stream of individual pilgrims, not a few from places far from Corps, was constant.

Reflecting on such reports, with their repeated references to the attention given the two children and the unremitting questioning to such they were subjected, Bishop de Bruillard decided that something should be done to protect the boy and girl. He implemented this decision in November on receipt of a letter from the watchful Father Mélin. The pastor of Grenoble told the bishop that a group of people from the diocese of Gap had proposed to take the children away to their town, provide them with a decent living, and see to their education. Father Mélin suspected and feared that this might be a flimsily disguised attempt to exploit Maximin and Melanie. His own idea was that the two should be sent to school to the Sisters of Providence in Corps, with Melanie living at the convent, and Maximin spending his days there. This plan the bishop found excellent, and it was put into effect, with the diocese of Grenoble paying whatever it might cost.

The convent at Corps was small, housing no more than four nuns, of whom Sister St. Thecla was the superior. The boy and girl were given a hearty welcome (which they liked), and set at school work (which they did not like). How much they had to learn, not least of all the many catechism lessons which must be mastered before reception of first holy Communion is permitted. Melanie was well past the usual age for first Communion, and Maximin was somewhat past it. They proved far from apt pupils. Memorizing was next to impossible for these two who could effortlessly repeat every word of the beautiful lady's discourse.

There were, of course, so many distractions, interruptions. The bishop had firmly ordered that during school hours the children were not to be disturbed by visitors. The order was hard to carry out. For, try though the sisters would to shield their charges, pilgrims to the place of the apparition would knock on the schoolroom door or barge in without knocking, demanding to see the pair. Should the sisters try to bar the way to these intruders, there were expostulations, recriminations. Had the strangers not come a great distance? Were they to have no consideration at all? Weren't they entitled to at least a look at the children, a word with them? It became known that Maximin was at the convent only during the day, so the visitors waited at the door for his emergence after a skull-cracking session at elusive lessons. When he stepped out, they swarmed around him, all but stifling him. Still others hung about Giraud's house, pre-empting the kitchen, squatting on the doorsill, making it difficult for Mme. Giraud to do her work or for any member of the family to get in or out. Giraud, though now so remarkably changed, could not reconcile himself to this insolence, this deprivation of privacy, this relentless hounding. But he bore them with the scant grace he could muster. There was worse in store for him in the spring.

In December the two commissions, that of the seminary professors and that of the cathedral canons, placed their reports before the bishop. Although these groups made separate examinations of the files concerning LaSalette, held separate discussions, and drew up separate reports, they were fully agreed in the opinion they submitted. They told the bishop that, to their minds, the best course was to watch and wait for some time yet. They could not, on the basis of the available material, form a decision either in favor of, or in opposition to, the authenticity of the event. There must be further clarification before a decision one way or the other could be reached. The commission of canons proposed that the bishop initiate a formal juridical inquiry. He thanked them for their labors, agreed with their findings, and resolved to institute a juridical inquiry in a few months.

The winter, with its screaming storms, greatly reduced the number of visitors to Corps and the mountain. Snow and ice and petrifying cold persuaded many planning pilgrimages to wait until milder weather came again. And so the children had some relief from being harried.

Some relief, but by no means complete relief. A few visitors braved the winter's castigation. And others had to come to Corps regardless of the state of the roads. One of the latter was Father Lagier, parish priest of St. Pierre de Chérennes, who was a native of Corps. In the winter of 1846-47 his father became mortally ill, and the son was called home. He stayed on in Corps for some time, and part of his leisure he determined to devote to interrogating Melanie and Maximin. He was not motivated by sympathy with the children. In fact, he put no credence in the story of the apparition, regarded the popular enthusiasm with distaste, thought the whole affair shady, and sought to stamp out what he considered the beginnings of a harmful legend. He had the great advantage of commanding the local patois, as other investigators did not.

He interviewed the children separately. His questioning of Melanie can justly be called fierce and might even be called ruthless. It went on for three sessions of at least five hours each. Maximin, though closely examined, got off easier. Perhaps the priest felt that if trickery was involved, as he suspected, Melanie, being considerably the older, was its originator and director, hence must be mercilessly hammered at. He was later to declare, "I am not afraid to admit that I began my sessions with the young herder in the hope of showing up a piece of imposture, having firmly decided to use every gift given me by God to embarrass, surprise, intimidate, frighten this child. I wanted to obtain a result, and I hoped that it would vindicate my original attitude."

He went over the same ground again and again, putting a question, dropping it, moving on to something else, suddenly rapping out the first question in a different form, telling the girl that earlier she had said something which she had not, incessantly trying to startle or terrify her into revealing the secret she maintained had been given her.

"And now you're going to tell me what the lady told you?"

"No."

"Surely you'll tell it to a priest like me whom you know and who is from your own town?"

"No."

"Why?"

"No, because . . ."

"Come, come. Why?"

"Oh—no!"

"You'll certainly tell it to a priest who can guard the secret well . . . ?"

"No, I am *not* going to tell it."

"Not to anyone at all?"

"I don't want to tell it."

"But to someone who is wise?"

"Wise or not wise, I don't want to tell it."

"You can."

"But I don't want to."

"And the reason?"

"I don't want to."

"Are you afraid that if you tell it to someone, he won't keep it strictly to himself?"

"Whatever he'd do, I don't want to tell it."

"But why?"

"Because I have been forbidden to tell it! I don't want to tell it, and I'm never going to tell it!"

"This secret of yours, does it concern heaven or hell?"

"It concerns whatever it concerns. If I tell you that, you'll know the secret, and I don't want to tell you."

"But without telling me what the secret is, you certainly could tell me whether it concerns religion or something else."

"Whatever it concerns, I don't want to tell it."

Fifteen hours of this grilling, but no hint of the contents of the secret, no deviation from the story as related from the start, no missteps into the snares craftily set by the interrogator. It was a tough experience for the girl, a tough test of her veracity and the authenticity of the story. Nowhere during it was there a chance for the sort of repartee which marked some of the question-and-answer bouts with other volunteer examiners. A priest from Gap, for example, had said to Melanie, "The lady disappeared in a cloud." Melanie had replied, "There wasn't any cloud." The priest had insisted, "But it's easy to be enveloped in a cloud and disappear." "Very well," said Melanie. "Wrap yourself in a cloud and disappear." Another priest had said to Maximin, "Don't you get tired repeating the same story day after day?" Maximin's answer was, "Do you get tired of saying the same Mass day after day?" But the tenacious Father Lagier couldn't be disposed of in that way. He attacked and attacked and attacked. If the children had begun this business for a lark or as a trick, they surely would have abandoned it once for all under this endless bombardment. They did not waver. Father Lagier marveled at their steadfastness, at the unshakable consistency of all they said. He did not vanquish them; they vanquished him. They did not give up their story; he gave up his doubt.

6

News of the happenings at LaSalette and Corps
reached Paris. In the anti-religious papers there were
distorted reports and scoffing comments. "A fantastic
imposture," was their common opinion, although the
writers gave no indication of having made any sort of
investigation. They felt they didn't have to: that is
manifestly a fraud which deals with a non-existent
being. The picture with verses, the unauthorized publication of which Bishop de Bruillard had tartly condemned, was widely circulated, in the capital as elsewhere. The government was displeased. Above all else,
it wanted the people to be quiet, to go meekly about
their appointed business. France was unsettled enough
without this new element of ferment. The story would
stir everybody up, draw people away from their accustomed routine, bring them together from all parts
of the country and thus give them an opportunity to
compare notes, exchange complaints and grievances.
Besides, some opportunist might seize on the story,
with its popular appeal, as a means to power.

Accordingly, stern word was sent from Paris that, at
all costs and as quickly as possible, the story was to be

scotched. The concocters of the pretended apparition
were to be found and punished. Those very words were
used, "pretended apparition," showing that the distant authorities had the same attitude of scientific
objectivity as the distant press. The order was directed
to the Royal Prosecutor at Grenoble. This dignitary, accompanied by two magistrates, made his uncomfortable way to Ablandins in the dead of winter, traveling
incognito. He called together Baptiste Pra and Pierre
Selme, put them under oath, raked them with questions. He carred away with him a copy of Pra's tran-
scription of the story told by Melanie. He would study
this, and they would hear from him again.

But when he acted, in the spring, it was through the
justice of the peace at Corps, who was directed to sum-
mon to his tribunal Melanie and Maximin as disturbers
of public order and to find out from them who had put
them up to their mischief. Since the justice of the peace
was away, his deputy, a man named Long, took the
matter in hand.

Giraud and his wife were frightened when the summons was announced, and so were the Mathieus. In
trouble with the law, this was too much, the last straw.
They went to see Father Mélin. The pastor had heard
that the authorities were convinced a priest was behind
the children's story. Very likely, he himself was suspected. He was not perturbed. Let them sieve the
affair as often and as strenuously as they would; it
would only serve to make the truth stand forth un-
impugnably. He quieted the anxious parents. No, he
would not accompany the children to the tribunal. "I
wouldn't be let in, anyhow," he told them, "and I'm
just as glad. You've nothing to worry about. The children won't be confounded. In fact, they'll do better by
themselves than if anyone tried to help them." The

Girauds and the Mathieus were reassured, and the girl and boy went bravely off to face the law.

This inquiry, surrounded with such legal trappings as Corps could supply, lasted six hours. Long quizzed the pair intensively, and the clerk of the court wrote down everything said, his pen scratching away over page after page. Each particular of the story was microscopically covered, and periodically Long would pleasantly interject a warning of the grievous penalties they could expect if caught out in a lie.

The next day Father Mélin chanced to meet the clerk of the court in the street. "Tell me," he said, "did your inquiry yesterday turn up anything new concerning the apparition?"

"No. But the Royal Prosecutor won't let it go at that. We've put everything together and sent it on to him."

"So much the better. If this thing is investigated as fully as possible, its truth or falsehood is bound to be clearly established. But look out for me. After the children, I'm the first who'll have to be brought to the bar of justice."

"Oh no," said the clerk. "Nobody believes you invented the story. However, there is suspicion of someone else. We have our eye on him."

"Would it be possible to know who this person is? Is it a priest?"

"Well, we've got to proceed slowly and carefully, otherwise we'd defeat our own purpose. But you're right. It is a priest."

"A priest of this district?"

"Yes, of this district."

"I'm astonished and embarrassed. Tell me who it is."

"All right, it's your neighbor in Ambel."

"Father R——?"

"Yes, he's the one."

"Thanks for letting me know. But be assured that my neighbor in Ambel puts even less credence in the apparition than you do yourself." This was the literal truth. The priest in question had declared that concerning the children's story he was completely neutral, neither accepting it nor rejecting it. He was content to let time set its value.

The deputy justice of the peace wrote to the prosecutor's office in Grenoble on May 23, 1847, saying, "I have the honor of sending on the statement made by the two children who told of the appearance of a lady unknown to them on the mountain of LaSalette-Fallavaux last September. This statement does not differ from what they told their employers when they got home on the evening of the day of the apparition. If there is any difference, it is in some words. But the essence is the very same." There were no legal steps taken; no one was brought to the bar of justice.

But the government tried another line. In June, the Minister of Justice and of Cults dictated in his handsomely appointed Paris office a letter to Bishop de Bruillard. It had been brought to his attention, he said, that there was being peddled in several parts of the country a picture supposed to be that of an apparition of the Virgin. Also, there were some statements, attached to the picture or separate, giving the details of this pretended apparition and a prediction of the great famine and a mortal sickness striking children. According to one of these statements, printed in Angers by the Widow Piguet, 14 St. Giles Street, an archbishop and two bishops were taken in by this wonder and sent word of it to Rome. "You will appreciate quite as well as I do," the minister had his secretary write to the bishop, "the danger posed by these publications, and you will not allow them to be sanctioned in any way by you. It is important, you will understand, to stop this evil thing in its tracks by telling the people the truth, and to thwart the blameworthy maneuvers whose success is the easier in that they make an appeal to religious sentiment."

If the bishop was annoyed when first he ran his eye over this remarkable composition, he must, seasoned as he was, have quickly managed a smile. Pomposity, gratuitous assumption, none too subtle innuendo sententiously stomped across the heavy, crested sheet. The minister treated the bishop as more than a little stupid and instructed him in the duties of his office as if the grand old man of eighty-one were a green cleric. One of the prelates allegedly taken in by the wonder was plainly himself, so much was broadly hinted. He was obliquely, but not very obliquely, accused of encouraging the publications of which the minister complained, and of complicity in forwarding an evil thing. The minister took it for granted that it was evil. Was not the apparition, for him, "this pretended apparition"? That evaluation he must have arrived at by intuition, for he had not tested the facts. Evidently, he had not even bothered to read the report from the deputy justice of the peace at Corps. Of course, one could understand that the authorities would be concerned lest the people panic when warnings of famine and pestilence were sounded. But might these gentlemen not go to the slight trouble required to ascertain that these warnings were conditional? *If* the people did not obey the law of God, punishment would follow. What was novel in that? What was evil in it? It made sense. Even pragmatically viewed, it was to the public benefit.

The bishop wrote a tactful reply.

"I do not know whether an archbishop and a bishop

93

have informed the court of Rome of the happening at LaSalette . . . For my part, I am entirely unacquainted with the communication in question, if it ever was made . . . I have not authorized any picture, account, or notice concerning the apparition. I have forbidden the episcopal printer, the only one over whom I have jurisdiction, to publish anything whatever having to do with this matter, and I am certain that he has obeyed my instructions.

"Hardly had I heard of the talk concerning the happening when I sent to my priests a letter in which I cited the article of my synodal statutes prohibiting the promulgation, without express authorization, of any new miracle. And all of them, with the exception of one imprudent man (a simple priest) obeyed the direction of their bishop.

"Still, this is a grave matter. My eyes and ears are trained on everything that is being said or done, everything that is happening.

"On my return from a long visitation of my diocese, I learned that, at the order of higher authority, the justice of the peace at Corps put the two little herders through a very long interrogation. I am told that, in their replies, they showed candor and poise which proved unshakable."

Spring, with its vivifying sun, had brought glossy green grass, sprinkled with the first of the year's wild-flowers, back to the mountain. It had also brought an ever larger number of pilgrims to trample grass and flowers in the place of the apparition. As the season gentled the mountain country, the number of visitors became greater. Some days as many as 600 people made their way to the famous ravine; 6,000 climbed there on May 31. There were reports of cures, either on the mountain or in distant towns and cities where ailing people were praying to Our Lady of LaSalette and using water from the spring now widely considered miraculous. It was at this time that some of the people took it on themselves to set up the Stations of the Cross along the path which the lady had taken through the ravine.

Obviously, interest in the apparition, far from dying out, was swelling. And this without any encouragement by the Church, without any authorized word in favor of the apparition. The Church's silence was calculated to be a brake on any runaway enthusiasm, but it did not stop the advance of curiosity, conviction, devotion.

It was on July 19, 1847, that Bishop de Bruillard began the juridical inquiry which was to last for four years. In announcing its inception, he said that he considered it his duty to make an investigation in the prescribed form. He cited certain factors demanding such a process. The first was the widespread preoccupation with the apparition; it had come to the notice of people not only in his own diocese and in neighboring dioceses, but all across France. Secondly, there were the numerous accounts of cures which some held to be miraculous, and which were at least astonishing. Thirdly, hundreds of people, clergy and laity, had written or personally called on him to register the firm belief in the apparition which possessed them after visiting the mountain and talking to Melanie and Maximin. Fourthly, he was being entreated to make an official pronouncement on the event; each day added to the appeals of this nature.

He was therefore delegating two of his priests to start the juridical inquiry in his name. One of these was a vicar general of the diocese, Father Rousselot, who had long been professor of theology in the Grenoble major seminary. This full-faced, white-haired priest, whose sharp eyes were framed by metal-rimmed spectacles, would become the official historian of LaSalette, producing, in a series of books, an exhaustive record of everything having to do with the subject. The other delegate was Father Orcel, superior of the major seminary and honorary canon of the cathedral, a lean-faced priest whose ascetic features were lighted by a benign smile. They had been chosen for their attributes of precision and patience in judgment. Doubtless the fact that, at the outset, Father Orcel was strongly and outspokenly unfavorable to the apparition counted in his choice. The bishop wanted the alleged occurrence to be put to the stiffest possible trial.

To that end, he directed the two delegates to associate with themselves in the inquiry such priests and laymen as were qualified to make it thorough and accurate. He laid special stress on consultation with the doctors who had treated those supposedly cured by invocation of Our Lady of LaSalette or after use of water from the once dried up spring. These medical men were to be asked for a history of such patients and an opinion on what, if anything, had happened to them after they had sought a miraculous cure.

Father Rousselot and Father Orcel began by visiting nine dioceses from which priests and people had come on pilgrimage to LaSalette and in which cures had been reported. It was tedious work, requiring constant traveling in the summer's heat and dust, looking up scores of persons, interviewing them, taking down what they had to say, and giving very careful consideration to the cases of those supposedly freed of some serious ailment through the intercession of the Blessed Virgin. Six bishops received the delegates and talked over at length with them the pros and cons of the matter.

After a month so occupied, they came to Corps. This meant still further questioning for the children. They were brought face to face with the bishop's interrogators one evening, and were separately examined. The next day, chilly and dark for midsummer, the two delegates went up to the mountain. The children were with them, and so were Father Mélin and Father Louis Perrin. Father Rousselot remarked on the rigors of this trip, which made the unabating ardor of the pilgrim crowds seem all the more imposing.

Their local priests had long since stood with Melanie and Maximin in this noble spot and heard their story. But now, for the first time, the Church was officially present in the ravine ringed with virgin peaks and ceilinged with virgin sky. Here, in the person of the bishop's delegates, the Church had come to scrutinize a story which concretized in the wayward nineteenth century what she had been teaching for almost two millennia, to analyze stringently events which seemed to speak resoundingly of heaven's mercy.

Having seen and heard what they would, and keeping their own counsel, Father Rousselot and Father Orcel climbed into the stage coach and headed for Grenoble.

When the first anniversary of the children's experience came round, on September 19, 1847, there was still no public indication of any opinion which the delegates might have formed. But they evidently had imparted a favorable impression to the bishop, for on this occasion he allowed the celebration of Mass at the site of the apparition. Well in advance of September 19, it was plain that that day would see such an assemblage at LaSalette as might rival the sum total of pilgrims during the year. Father Louis Perrin arranged for the erection of a covered altar. As the day drew near he converted it into a double altar, so that two Masses might be celebrated simultaneously, thus giving as many as possible an opportunity to witness, as well as assist in, the Holy Sacrifice.

On September 16, the vanguard arrived. September 17 saw the roads choked with others. Corps, La-Salette, Ablandins, though they had grown accustomed to visitors since last September, had never known anything like this mass invasion. The priests there and in surrounding towns spent almost all their waking hours in the confessional. By the hundreds, by the thousands, the pilgrims demanded to receive the sacraments. Every hour saw the churches crowded. Any corner which might do as a lodging was taken days ahead. People slept in kitchens, in hallways, in barns, in stables. And some had to sleep in the open.

Those arriving on Saturday, the 18th, saw that it was no use trying to get under a roof anywhere in the vicinity. They decided to spend the night on the mountain. It was raining heavily, and because of the storm darkness set in early. This made the ascent of the mountain hazardous indeed, but no one would turn back. Many there were who slipped and fell or lost their way on the unfamiliar paths. When the destination was reached, there was no protection against the elements. The scene of the apparition lay nakedly open to the furious storm. As the winds ricocheted fiercely off the high Alps, as the lashing torrents beat down relentlessly, the people huddled together in the desolate darkness, cold, soaked through, hungry. Someone began the recitation of prayers, the singing of hymns. They sounded faint against the shrieking gale. But the crowd took up the responses, joined in the chant, and the storm's clamor was in some measure offset. At 2:30 in the morning, candles were lighted on the sheltered altars. The flames, valiantly battling the wind, cheered the sodden throng. Mass was begun, a priest at each altar. Hundreds of drenched men, women, and children slithered across the muddy ground to kneel for a moment under the improvised roof and receive Communion. When the first two Masses were finished, others commenced; and so it went until almost noon, a ceaseless series of Masses, where no Mass had ever previously been offered.

Before the break of day, those on the mountain could see that other pilgrims were moving toward the heights. Their approach was signaled by the wind-flattened blaze of the torches they carried. Long, wavering lines of light crawled up the mountain. Through the howling blasts there rose the prayers of the newcomers. Every hour brought more. Around ten o'clock the rain ceased, the clouds were swept away, and the sun burst blindingly in sight. The night's ordeal was forgotten. Joy rang across the mountainside as the voices of the teeming multitude took on the bright quality which the day had just assumed. Around the altars the crowd was packed solid, tens of thousands with hardly room to move a hand. At about noon, a priest spoke to the people. His voice was strong, resonant, as he described the happening of September 19, 1846. But his words were lost to many who could not get near enough to hear. Another priest spoke. Then word was sent around that the assemblage should divide into two groups, one on the right side of the ravine, the other on the left. When, slowly and with difficulty, this separation had been effected, the *Magnificat* was intoned. One half of the throng would sing one verse, the other half the next.

Thus they went through several of the great prayers associated with our Lady, and finally they alternated in the *Te Deum*, that stately, expansive, cumulatively thrilling proclamation of the praises of God which runs the gamut of creation and has immemorially been the Christian form of most solemn thanksgiving.

What could Maximin and Melanie have thought of it? They were on hand, Maximin escorted by his father, Melanie by the nuns from Corps. How different a scene from twelve months ago! Then this place was empty of all save themselves, a few cows, Selme in the near distance, the three other herders in the far distance. Then there was stillness unbroken save by their own voices, the tinkle of a cowbell, the thin, treble clangor of the Angelus bell. But now! Fifty or sixty thousand people standing in line for five or six hours to get near the bubbling spring which a year back had given no water. A din of voices in conversation, a thundering of voices in prayer. Dozens of Masses. Where then only the beautiful lady spoke to them, now an interminable line of people addressed them, shot questions at them, caressed them, plucked at their clothes, pulled them this way and that. Someone got the idea that they should repeat their story as the most suitable way of observing the anniversary. This they did, saying a sentence or two at a time, then pausing while a leather-lunged stalwart shouted it out to those in the background, and yet another relayed it further, and still another. At its finish, the suggestion was made that the boy and the girl lead the pilgrims in the Rosary. When the last *"Ave"* had been said, the children, tired and in danger of being crushed, were led away. The great day was over.

In October, Father Rousselot and Father Orcel made their report to the bishop. Father Rousselot later incorporated it in his first book on LaSalette, published in 1849. Here was no casual, superficial ticking off of the pertinent data, but a systematic and exacting inspection which studied every particular, faced every possible alternative to the conclusion that the children had told the truth, and proceeded with unexceptionable logic to an affirmation of belief in the reality of what they reported.

The delegates found altogether extraordinary the unshatterable consistency of the children's story. Over a period of many months they had been required to retell it times beyond computing and in various circumstances. They had been interrogated by astute adults, some of them skilled in courtroom practice, many of them using wiles and stratagems likely to detect any lie or variation. On one of the occasions when the two were separately quizzed, Melanie was confronted with a woman and asked whether the beautiful lady was taller or shorter than this person. She immediately replied, "taller." Then Maximin, without even seeing Melanie, was asked the same question; his prompt response was "taller." From September to December, 1846, Melanie was at Ablandins, Maximin in Corps. They were queried almost daily. Far apart though they were, they gave identical replies. And they showed no nervousness, no fear lest they be caught out or contradict each other. They went straightforwardly through their recital, answered inquiries directly, were never ruffled. They showed apprehension only when someone mercilessly pressed and chivied them for the revelation of their secrets.

That they had invented the whole thing was inconceivable. Feature after feature of it was beyond their ken. Of religion they were appallingly ignorant; it simply did not figure in their lives. The persons, the doctrines standing out in the story were unknown to them. The beautiful lady's costume, which they described so meticulously, was of a sort totally unfamiliar to them, and its most significant details they could not appreciate. That they could fluently repeat a long discourse in French was hardly short of dumbfounding, since of this language they knew next to nothing.

The delegates were satisfied that the children were neither deceived nor deceivers. All the sure tests of hallucination failed in their case, and that they were not the victims of a hoax was established both by the continuous and incisive inquisition to which they had been put and by examination of the scene of their experience. As for their being deceivers, this would mean either that they made up the story (which was demonstrably untenable) or that they were coached by someone else (of which no jot of evidence could be found in unremitting canvasses of the affair).

Emphasis was put on the reluctant but unanimous acceptance of the story as true by the people best situated to refute it from the start. These were the folk of Ablandins and LaSalette. They had it from Maximin and Melanie at once, the people of Ablandins directly after the alleged happening, the people of LaSalette the next day. Hardly was it out of the children's mouths, when disbelief in it was voiced, roughly, scornfully. Since Maximin and Melanie would not be budged, they were cross-examined, laughed at, threatened. Their hearers were grossly incredulous, inimical to marvel-mongering. Yet they had been compelled to accept the story.

Then there was the conviction of people from afar. They had come, seen, spoken to the children, credited something which they had been predisposed to reject. Some of them were doctors, some lawyers, some members of other professions: that is, educated men, trained to scan evidence, acquainted with the vagaries of the human mind, slow and gingerly in reaching conclusions.

The report also called attention to twenty-three cures which had followed upon an appeal to Our Lady of LaSalette. One, for example, was in the case of a nun certified to have been in an advanced state of tuberculosis and to be now wholly well. Notable, too, was the improvement in Christian living which had taken place in the diocese and elsewhere.

The delegates expressed their own acceptance of "the extraordinary event of LaSalette" as verified and said that priests and people awaited the doctrinal judgment of Bishop de Bruillard. The bishop was still in no hurry. After reading the report, he appointed a commission of sixteen priests, men outstanding (as he put it) for their balance, piety, and learning, to consider it and meet with him for a series of discussions. This group, held to secrecy, comprised his two vicars general, the head of the major seminary, the eight cathedral canons, and the five parish priests of Grenoble. They met eight times between November 8 and December 13, 1847, talked over the report sentence by sentence, debated crucial points, examined the two children. The bishop presided at these sessions, but said little, allowing the priests complete freedom to speak their minds and thresh out every phase of the subject. At the last meeting he announced that the discussions were now ended, thanked the participants, and promised a doctrinal judgment at a suitable time. Four of the priests did not go along with the majority's approval of the report, and one of these was to make considerable trouble in the years ahead.

7

With their appearances before the ecclesiastical tribunal in Grenoble, Melanie and Maximin moved from the center of the stage in the story of LaSalette. They had done what they had been told to do. They had communicated the beautiful lady's words to the people, with results already visible. They had communicated her words to the Church, and the Church, having studiously examined the messengers as well as the message, was now, in the person of the local bishop, crystallizing a judgment. The children's task was finished, as they themselves realized and said.

But interest in them, widespread and acute as it had become, did not now die down. People still wanted to see them, wanted to know everything about their doings. As long as they lived, they would be linked with LaSalette, and each phase of their careers from the present until death would be observed and used as an index of the worth of the apparition. Instead of focussing on the event itself as painstakingly established, or on the character and consequences of devotion to Our Lady of LaSalette to determine the value of that devotion, many would judge LaSalette solely by the subsequent conduct of the two who made the original announcement and thereafter were to step aside, their assigned role discharged.

Great had been their privilege on that September day in 1846, and great was the payment for it required of them before they could attain the only privacy and peace which would be theirs, the privacy of the grave and the peace of eternity. If they were witnesses, they may also be said to have been victims. If they had seen Our Lady of Sorrows, they would themselves never be free of sorrows until they went to her in the everlasting mountains as she had come to them in the mountains beyond Corps. They would suffer almost without interval. They would be homeless, as if a glimpse of the glory which is the human destination deprived them of earthly rest and roots.

One of their worst trials was that not a few people expected of them that they be saints, nothing less. These mistook the call to perform a specific service with the guarantee of a special sanctity. Though the children were far from brilliant or learned, they at least discerned the difference. Melanie clung stoutly to her story of the event on the mountain, but when a woman asked for some little belonging of hers by which to remember her, the girl replied, "I don't want anyone to remember me. I am not a saint, and people shouldn't be thinking of me." And when another woman asked her whether, looking at the swiftly scattering light where the beautiful lady had been but a moment before, she had not believed that she herself would surely be a saint, the answer was a regretful "No." It was an answer the true and tragic sense of which only the thinking few would perceive.

The four years, from 1846 to 1850, which the children spent as charges of the nuns in the plain little convent at Corps, were by no means a period of placid retirement. The boy and girl were seldom let alone, and the nuns always had their hands full. There were the visitors; never a day without these. There were the jubilant reports of miracles. There were the trips to the mountain. There were the trips to the bishop's house in Grenoble. And there was the almost yieldless labor of trying to teach two children who so long had gone untaught and showed so little aptitude for learning. Day in, day out, Sister St. Thecla worked with Melanie, endeavoring to have the girl memorize the Acts of Faith, Hope, and Charity. Day in, day out she strove to help Maximin master the not very difficult requisites for serving Mass. Her patience, and that of the other nuns, was monumental. So was their discretion.

It was the rule that the apparition was never the subject of conversation or questioning. But, inevitably, sometimes it came unbidden into the talk at recreation. Thus, when Maximin, whom the sisters called "Perpetual Motion" because of his habitual fidgeting, once had to be chided for his ill manners, Melanie said with a sniff that he had been ill mannered even in the presence of the Blessed Virgin.

"How is that?" one of the sisters said sharply. "He didn't behave well in *her* presence? Why, what did he do?"

"Well, he kept his hat on when first she was speaking to us. Then he took his hat off, put it on his staff, and twirled it around."

Was this true? Maximin muttered that it was. But when Melanie added that he had knocked some stones along the ground toward the beautiful lady, he angrily corrected her. "It was only one stone," he said, "and, anyhow, it couldn't touch her."

This flare-up between the children was nothing exceptional. They did not particularly care for each other, and they were in agreement about almost nothing save the facts and the details of the apparition. When Maximin spoke of becoming a priest and going to a pagan land as a missionary, it was suggested that, since Melanie wished to become a nun and do mission work, she could accompany and assist him. "Melanie can go where she likes," he replied, "but it won't be with me!" Another time, at odds with Melanie, he said, "You'll see! When I'm a priest and you come to confession to me, I'll give you such a penance that you'll never want to come back." "If you're waiting for me to go to your confessional," Melanie answered, "I can tell you that you'll have an empty box!"

Regularly, the nuns witnessed these instances of conflict. They could only wonder the more that the children agreed so perfectly as to what had happened on the mountain that September day in 1846, and also that they unfailingly did the same thing when some visitor overrode their refusal of money gifts—they at once turned these over to Sister St. Thecla. For the rest, there was hourly, patent, and occasionally even painful evidence of the differences between them, differences which made it impossible to think of them as co-conspirators, much less successful co-conspirators, in perpetrating an intricate, sustained deception. Surely, were there any trickery, it would come out in these passages-at-arms.

The children's basic difference was one of temperament, as the nuns could observe in daily contact with them. Their respective histories had served to accentuate their original dissimilarity. Maximin was cheerful, sportive, uninhibited. He liked people, enjoyed the company of almost anyone, reveled in comings, goings, bustle, excitement. But Melanie was shy, guarded, fearful, one might almost say morose at times. She was withdrawn and mute in the presence of others, especially strangers, and all the to-do following upon the apparition displeased and sometimes frightened her. Where Maximin would chatter away to a visiting bishop, tug at his sash, poke at his ring and his pectoral cross, dance around him to inspect his robes, Melanie would stand wordlessly by, hands clasped, head a little lowered. Often, she seemed to move in a dream. Now and then she startled someone in the convent by saying that she wished to die. "But why," she was asked.

"Because I don't like to stay on earth."

"And why is that?"

"Because . . . because it's too . . . ugly!"

"You would like to go where you could again see that beautiful, shining lady?"

"Ah, yes, yes!"

Eighteen months elapsed between the time of their being put in the Sisters' care and their reception of first Communion. It took a year and a half of instruction to prepare them for something that was long past for their contemporaries. Then there were two more years of studying religion before they were confirmed. But, though learning the catechism came hard to them, something of the spirit and practice of piety were more easily acquired. For two to whom religion had, in the most impressionable years, meant hardly anything, they were gratifyingly devout. But, again, with a difference. Melanie's devotion had a brooding quality; it was unsmiling, touched with sadness. Maximin resorted to prayer and the sacraments gaily and without serious concentration.

It was remarked that the children did not give themselves airs even when thousands of pilgrims asked to see them and treated them with reverence. Melanie evinced no delight when a pilgrim spoke of her as "the Blessed Virgin's little girl." She only shrugged exasperatedly when another exclaimed, "Look at that crowd of people! You are the one who brought them all here." When still another asked her to put her arms around a child and thus effect the cure of its speech defect, Melanie drew back, her eyes flashing indignation, and refused, despite repeated pleas, to touch the child. She knew that curing people was not in her power. More than once she said she wished she had not been commanded to make known the message given her, for all the people, in the ravine. She was asked why. "Because," she replied, "it puts me too much on exhibition." Yet the possibility that Melanie might in time be affected by the ceaseless attention showered on her troubled Sister St. Thecla. Although the child now gave no indication of being carried away by the regard and the flattery lavished on her, the nun speculated on the cumulative effect of such treatment. She had some reason for this concern, as the event would disclose. As for the volatile, unintrospective Maximin, much more used as he was to people and popularity, there was little danger of his being carried away.

Melanie could be curt in disposing of the inquiries which people were forever addressing to her. She would radiate joy when describing the apparition; the time so spent was her happiest. But the casual visitors' heckling might strike a fiery spark. One of these, failing to elicit the secret given Melanie, said, "Well, you'll certainly have to tell it to the priest when you go to confession before your first Communion." She answered with acerbity, "My secret is no sin, therefore I won't have to tell it in confession." When a priest, careless of the truth, told her, "God has revealed your secret to a holy nun. But I'd rather have it from you, so as to be convinced that you're not lying." "As long as this nun knows it," said Melanie, "she can tell it to you. I won't."

Maximin, too, could be nettled. A man who was quizzing him remarked, "If the Blessed Virgin had wanted to speak to children, she would have chosen some who were good, really pious, really pure of heart."

"How do you know, sir, that I am not pure of heart?"

An excellent question; his interlocutor slyly shifted ground. "Because you scandalized me this morning by your giddiness while serving Mass. You turned your head. If the Blessed Virgin had ever appeared to you, you would have been more recollected."

"Very well. I'm not steady. That's all that amounts to."

"You and Melanie are in cahoots. Someone gave you money to tell this yarn."

"All right. If you know so much, sir, tell me the amount of money I got."

The question was dodged. "I simply can't believe you. How can you ask me to have any faith in you?"

"Sir, I don't ask you to have any faith in me, but only in what happened."

It was not only this unnamed gentleman who withheld credence. Four of the sixteen priests on the board named by Bishop de Bruillard to consider the report of Father Rousselot and Father Orcel in 1847 had voted against approval of it, as was their right and, indeed, if honest conviction dictated a negative vote, their duty. One of the four, Father Cartellier, became the promoter of an opposition movement of little weight but great bitterness and even viciousness.

Those participating in the discussions at the bishop's house had been required to pledge that they would keep secret everything about those sessions. But reports of the proceedings began to leak out. The reports were far from reliable, yet there were in them enough accurate particulars to make it clear that someone involved in the discussions was circulating a selective and slanted account of them. The someone was the proud and disgruntled Cartellier.

He gradually showed that he would stop at nothing to discredit LaSalette, or, more precisely, to prove that he alone was right in the face of redoubtable evidence to the contrary. He maneuvered artfully to give the impression that there were serious objections to the acceptability of the children's story, but never cited any. He could not demonstrate fraud or lying; he could not show the story to be unacceptable by the rules of evidence. All he could do was drop hints, make pinpricks, strike glancing blows. But at this he was clever and persistent. When, in 1848, Father Rousselot published his first book on LaSalette, *The Truth Concerning the Event of LaSalette*, Father Cartellier anonymously published a book casting aspersions on the vicar general's work. He continued this anonymous assault in print, going so far as to distribute scurrilous printed attacks at the retreat for diocesan priests. Bishop de Bruillard was almost excessively forbearing in the face of such tactics, as well as an attempt to go over his head to the Cardinal Archbishop of Lyon, even though insinuations as to his own sanity figured in them.

Further opposition came from a gifted but contumacious priest of the diocese, Father Déléon, with whom the bishop had already had trouble. This man, pastor at Villeurbanne, was among the early believers in the apparition and had been responsible for many of his parishioners' going to the scene on pilgrimage. But when, in 1849, the bishop was forced to suspend him because of grave dereliction, he took his revenge by recklessly inveighing against LaSalette. He published

112

an unscrupulously contrived book, which Bishop de Bruillard called, "infamous . . . full of false allegations, lying assertions, and gross abuse of people who are beyond reproach."

Déléon's utterly unprincipled methods were most amazingly evidenced in his elaborate account of how, according to him, the alleged apparition had been staged. The children had not seen the Blessed Virgin, he said, but had been taken in by a certain Mlle. de Lamerlière. There was such a person, a woman in her late fifties who rejoiced in the imposing name of Constance Louise Marguerite Saint-Ferréol de Lamerlière. She was of illustrious family and ample fortune—and ample figure. For some years she had been in the convent, as a Sister of Providence, but her pronounced eccentricities made impossible her continuing as a religious. These eccentricities did not disappear with her return to the world. She was interminably at war with the members of her own family, and lawsuits seem to have been her favorite recreation. However, she was a most generous person, and her gifts to, and work for, charity were quite out of the ordinary.

Déléon cast her as the beautiful lady. According to him, she had for some time been in search of a scheme to make upon the heedless world an impression at once astonishing and inspiring. In the summer of 1846, he said, she had a flash of inspiration which she at once acted upon. She caused a costume to be made: a splendid white dress strewn with brilliants, a yellow apron, a shawl trimmed with roses and a chain, a cross, a hammer, and a pair of pliers (all of these in gold), fine slippers trimmed with roses, and a headdress similarly trimmed. She liked the results so well that she had the costume duplicated in blue and again in rose. All this finery, said Déléon, she packed, and then set out for Grenoble. From Grenoble she went up into the mountains, spied out the country above Ablandins, and finally hit on the spot and the circumstances of the feat she had in mind, as well as the costume, of the three, which she would wear. On Saturday, September 19, Déléon continued, she suddenly burst upon the dazzled eyes of Melanie and Maximin. And that was all there was to this jabbering about an appearance of our Lady.

But not quite all. For one thing, Mlle. de Lamerlière was hardly beautiful. For another, she was undisguisably fat. People got to laughing when they thought of someone fat and nearing sixty trudging unguided and unobserved up a mountain and over very difficult terrain, while encumbered with parcels containing an extensive wardrobe. How could a figure so considerable and so burdened have escaped notice? And where would she retire to array herself in her complex finery and to wait the propitious moment to make an entrance that would bowl the children over? There was no shelter, no screening for these essential parts of the Déléon scenario. Furthermore, Mlle. de Lamerlière did not speak a word of the local patois. But, more arresting still, was the proved fact that Mlle. de Lamerlière had not stirred out of the town of St. Marcellin, where she made her home, on September 18, September 19, September 20. In fact, on the day of the apparition she had been right in the midst of one of her accustomed processes at law in St. Marcellin—seventy miles from La-Salette. It was doubtful that she had the power of bilocation.

Father Déléon's malicious and outrageous fiction was blown to bits by a gale of ridicule. But it had some uncomic consequences. The incensed Mlle. de Lamerlière brought its author into court for the injury

114

he had done her by fabricating and spreading this lie. Though his story was exposed as false and impossible, it still lodged in some minds as perhaps having something to it after all. And skeptics were delighted with it. In a supposedly scholarly work which has undoubtedly hurt the religious faith of many, Solomon Reinach's *Orpheus,* Déléon's completely exploded invention is solemnly cited as proving the incident at La-Salette to have been a hoax and a classic example of clerical trickery.

Father Déléon did not continue in this pernicious way until the end of his life. He retracted his lies, admitted his wrongdoing, and before his death, at the age of 97, said, "I never rejected the fact of the apparition. It was just that I was against the bishop. I believed that he had mistreated me in giving me a position not in keeping with my merits." He struck at his bishop by striking at the one who wept on the mountain.

Four years at the convent school were enough for Maximin. The confinement became intolerable for the once foot-loose boy, and exclusively feminine company he found cloying. Such tame exploits as bringing a sheep into the convent and encouraging it to race about the rooms knocking things over were treated as capital calamities and crimes. Besides, being under official surveillance and endless questioning was irksome. He had now lost his father. Giraud's holy death brought edification to all; it was one of the unmistakable fruits of LaSalette. But to Maximin it brought loneliness; for him it broke a last tie to family. With Giraud, his home was gone. An uncle became the boy's guardian. This man's intentions were good, but he and Maximin never hit it off well.

Maximin ran away. He did not go far, nor was he

away long. But from this moment there dates the decades-long process of running away in which he would be engaged until he ran away from earth. He could not endure being tied down. He had thought, and would think again, of being a priest, but a priest moving over the world at will, not fixed in any one place. He now ran away in search of the freedom he had formerly enjoyed. He slipped through the winding streets of Corps, headed into the open country where the turf was springy under flying feet, took the road to Ablandins.

When he reached the hamlet so charged with memories for him, he was tired, hungry, dirty. He went up to the door of the Pras' house, that door at which he had rapped so gleefully on the morning of a day that was to prove fateful. He peered into the kitchen. Grandmother Pra was at work there. She was unaware of his presence for a while; then, looking up and seeing him, she did not at once recognize him. After a moment she said, "Oh, is that you, Maximin? Where have you come from? Are you sick? You're very pale, my child. Come in, come in!"

He went in. The old woman sat him at the scrubbed table and hurriedly got him something to eat. When he had wolfed down the impromptu meal, she asked him what was the matter, why he was here. He told her, in his most knowing manner, that he had left Corps for good, that he wanted to stay in Ablandins and work for his keep and a bit of money now and again. The money, he confided, would be for good times with his friends.

The Pras took him in and set him to work. For a few days he was able to relish the changed existence he had sought, the rough-and-ready life so unlike the decorousness and primly ordered routine of the convent.

But Baptiste Pra wondered whether he was doing right in keeping the boy, and on market day brought him down to Corps. There his disappearance had caused a sensation, and his return did hardly less.

He did not go back to the convent. His uncle strove valiantly to locate him suitably in this place and that. These efforts came to nothing. Maximin was at loose end when there was cooked up the project of having him go to visit the Curé of Ars, the internationally celebrated John Baptist Vianney. This scheme was to bring heartache to many, not least of all the saintly priest, who had, with groans and tears, rid his parish of many of the evils of which the tearful Lady of LaSalette had complained.

The ill-starred journey to Ars took place in 1850. In 1848, France had undergone yet another revolution, and another republic had been instituted. In spite of this, a nobleman whose title was Baron de Richemont, but who claimed the throne of France as Louis XVII, was surrounded at Lyon by a small, devoted, and avidly intriguing court. The little group was anxious to have their man come to power, and were ready to use almost any means to that end. It occurred to one of them that perhaps the children of LaSalette could help. Might not the pair be persuaded to say that the secret communicated to them during the apparition had to do with "Louis XVII," and recommended or predicted that he should rule the country? Get hold of the children, that was the thing to do.

One of de Richemont's partisans, a man named Bonafous, went to LaSalette for the fourth anniversary of the apparition. He found there three men who were interested in having Maximin go to Ars to ask the renowned curé whether or not he should become a Marist religious, as had been suggested. These three were sincerely concerned for Maximin's good; they had shown themselves his friends; they had no political connections or concerns. But they made common cause with Bonafous: the two proposed trips would be combined with visits to both Lyon and Ars. Bonafous tried to get Melanie to come along, but she gave him the slip. Maximin agreed to their proposal, since, as he said, it would give him an opportunity to see the world.

The men brought Maximin to Ars, arriving on the evening of September 24. The curé was not then available. He was in the confessional, where he spent most of his time. But they did see Father Raymond, the curé's assistant. This meeting was the lighted fuse to all the trouble which followed.

Father Raymond had now been in Ars for five years, five years which were terrible for the curé and those closest to him. The assistant had been forty years of age when assigned to the parish, some twenty years the junior of Father Vianney. The latter was by then famous all over the world, and to the town and to his confessional there flocked people from many countries. He was held in veneration by great churchmen in France and elsewhere. But the new assistant approached him with no awe at all.

Father Raymond was vigorous and good-looking. He fancied himself as an exceptional preacher and administrator. He was sure that in intelligence, learning, and wisdom he far surpassed the pastor so fortunate as to have him around. Ars, he believed, needed someone like him to bring order out of the perpetual tumult. And the curé, he felt, needed someone like him (could there be another?) to direct and correct him.

The assistant began by appropriating Father Vianney's room in the rectory. Since the curé was so much in church and slept so little, the damp and dingy downstairs cubbyhole surely would be all right for him. The bigger, brighter, more airy room upstairs should go to his bigger, brighter, more airy junior. It did. Although the curé had paid Father Raymond's way through the seminary, the young man did not hesitate to sign himself on the parish books and on any documents as "pastor," as if the curé had been officially superseded. He kept a close check on the curé, demanding an account of his day as well as an outline of anything he might have in mind to do. If he found the account not to his taste, he called the curé down. If the curé's plans did not meet his approval, he forbade their execution. He would listen critically to the curé's sermons, and when the preacher who moved more hearts and fired more souls than almost anyone in history had finished, Father Raymond would ponderously mount the pulpit to contradict whatever displeased him. The curé never objected; his humility and meekness were such that he took no offense. But some of the people of Ars took steps to see that Father Raymond was in some measure curbed. For example, he was required to let the pastor have his own room again, and eventually he took quarters in town, leaving the rectory to the curé.

As in most other things, Father Raymond disagreed with the curé's attitude toward LaSalette. The curé believed in the apparition. He had a lithographed picture of it in his house. He blessed religious articles representing the beautiful lady's meeting with the children. He used water from LaSalette. He encouraged people to go there on pilgrimage. Father Raymond, on the other hand, would not grant that there was any truth to the story. His reason seems to have been, according to his own word, that when once he went to LaSalette and met Maximin, the boy refused to answer his questions. If, on that occasion, the priest had shown his accustomed brusque and choleric manner, it may have alienated Maximin and caused him to refuse to be interrogated. In any case, Father Raymond was unfavorably disposed to the lad, and now, on the evening of September 24, 1850, it was to Father Raymond that Maximin was brought.

The curé's assistant made no attempt to hide his feelings. He pitched into Maximin, pelting him with questions bristling with animus. The substance of what he had to say was, not to put too fine a point on it, that LaSalette was a fiction and Maximin a liar. At length, Maximin said, "You'll have it your way. If you suppose that I actually saw nothing, then you'll call me a liar." The heated interview ended on that note, and Father Raymond informed the curé that the boy had as much as admitted that he was a liar.

The next morning, before seven o'clock, Maximin was brought to see the curé in the sacristy, near the confessional to which priests came as penitents. In the filtered morning light they faced each other, the gaunt, toothless, bent old man with the long white hair, and the fresh-faced, high-strung boy with the saucy eyes. Maximin said later that it was hard for him to understand the curé, who, in truth, was not too easy to understand because the loss of his teeth interfered with clear speech. The boy asked the pastor of Ars about going to the Marists and was strongly advised to return to his own diocese and do as his bishop thought best. When the curé asked him whether he had seen the Blessed Virgin, as reported, Maximin replied that he had seen a beautiful lady, but whether or not it was the Blessed Virgin he did not know. It appears that the curé, already having had to listen to Father Raymond's diatribe, misconstrued this answer. What Maximin had said was, in fact, exquisitely right: he had, indeed, seen a beautiful lady, but it was necessary to await the doctrinal decision of the Bishop of Grenoble before one could properly assert that the lady was the Blessed Virgin. But the curé interpreted his words as a denial that he had seen anyone at all, as an admission that there was no apparition. The curé wanted to know whether the boy had told lies in the past. Yes, was Maximin's answer, he had occasionally lied to Father Mélin, his pastor in Corps. This, too, was a truthful reply which cast no shadow on the apparition, for Maximin referred to lies which he had told Father Mélin when, as he put it, "I did not wish to tell him where I was going, or when I did not want to learn my lessons." But the curé concluded that LaSalette was a fraud, and this caused him bitter suffering.

At the end of this meeting, fifteen or twenty minutes in length but destined to have dire repercussions, Maximin was taken away to Lyon, where he met the would-be Louis XVII. He was badgered to declare that the lady of the apparition had confided to him a message helpful to the pretender's cause. He laughed, denied the suggestion, and said that he knew nothing of any Louis, whether sixteenth, seventeenth, or eighteenth. A fiasco for de Richemont's party. Maximin went back to Corps.

Some weeks later, the bumptious Father Raymond took it on himself to write a long letter to his ordinary, Bishop Devie, and sent copies to the Cardinal Archbishop of Lyon and the Bishop of Gap, both of whom he had reason to believe doubtful of the authenticity of the bruited apparition. He asserted flatly that Maximin had made a retraction to the curé, admitting that he was a liar and that the apparition story was a falsehood. Moreover, the curé had stopped speaking of La-Salette, refused any longer to bless religious articles in any way connected with it, and said of Maximin, "I was dissatisfied with him, and he was dissatisfied with me."

Bishop de Bruillard was thunderstruck. A retraction by Maximin after all the grilling he had been put through for four years without ever being shaken? Cartellier, Déléon, and such followers as they had were overjoyed. They were vindicated at last! All along they had maintained what an acknowledged saint had now brought into the daylight. The Curé of Ars had given the coup de grâce to the LaSalette legend, and all the dignitaries of the Grenoble diocese, credulous victims of a sorry swindle, were covered with disgrace. Their hoots of derision were relayed through France.

But Bishop de Bruillard did not retreat. He had Maximin examined by a commission composed of priests and layfolk. The boy reaffirmed the actuality of the apparition, insisted that he had made no denial of it to Father Vianney, and explained the misunderstanding. Then the bishop send Father Rousselot and Father Mélin to Ars to see the curé, but they were given little time and no satisfaction. A letter from Bishop de Bruillard to the curé drew a non-committal reply. An appeal to the curé's own bishop brought a letter in which Bishop Devie said that the curé had no competence to judge the truth or falsity of LaSalette, that Father Raymond had undoubtedly handled the boy roughly, and that any decision as to the authenticity of the apparition was Bishop de Bruillard's province and no one else's. He added that two other bishops, then his guests, joined him in the opinion that everything pointed to the reality of an appearance of the Blessed Virgin to the children.

The storm over what was to become known as "the Ars incident," blew for years. In 1851, Bishop de Bruillard would indicate that, in his considered judgment, it had not in the least overthrown the fact of the apparition. Backing for this would be supplied later by none other than the Curé of Ars himself.

Father Vianney said that his abandonment of credence in LaSalette caused him protracted torment. He grieved over it, and for eight years the subject kept coming up in his mind and disturbing him. "You will never know," he told a friend, "what agonies my soul has endured because of this. I suffered in a way that defies description. To get some idea, imagine a man in a desert, in the midst of a fierce sand storm, not knowing where to turn."

This torture of heart ceased only when, after some years, he made a firm act of faith in Our Lady of La-Salette. "I was at peace once more," he said, "I was as light as a bird, I could fly!" He had put Our Lady of LaSalette to the test in this wise. He was in need of money for the foundation of a mission. He prayed to the Blessed Virgin, under the title of Our Lady of LaSalette, to procure it for him, naming the exact amount required. That exact amount was promptly given him. "I firmly believe in LaSalette," he now told everyone he could reach. "I have been represented as not believing in it. On the contrary, I am a firm believer in it. That boy and I did not understand each other. But I have asked heaven for signs to shore up my faith, and I have had them. I tell you, one can and one *must* believe in LaSalette."

Thus was removed one more obstacle—and, to many, the most forbidding—in the way of general acceptance of the apparition as genuine. But the process of removal, wholly successful though it was, proved slow and painful.

Shortly after his return from the journey to Ars, Maximin entered the minor seminary at Grenoble, to begin his studies for the priesthood. In that same autumn of 1850, Melanie left Corps for the convent of the Sisters of Providence at Corenc. She wanted to become a nun.

8

Cardinal de Bonald of Lyon was, as Father Raymond surmised, uninclined to credit the apparition at La-Salette. But, like many a less eminently placed person, he was curious about the secrets. Unlike many a less eminently placed person, he felt sure he could learn their contents. When Father Rousselot wrote to him to protest the extensive circulation of Father Raymond's letter, Cardinal de Bonald replied rather loftily, "I have not been concerned with the affair of LaSalette except for the respectful request (of which you doubtless know) I addressed to the Bishop of Grenoble in connection with the provincial council at Lyon. Now, however, I must concern myself with it in my capacity as consultor to the Pope. Hence I am asking you if Marcellin and his sister will confide their famous secrets to me in order that I may pass these on to His Holiness."

The turning of the phrase "their famous secrets" broadly indicated the writer's patronizing attitude. And the designation of Maximin as "Marcellin," and of Melanie as Maximin's anonymous sister, more than broadly indicated the writer's lack of familiarity with the rudiments of the matter of LaSalette. In the sentence containing the request to be apprised of the secrets, there were two references to the Holy Father; surely the recipient of the letter was meant to conclude that this request had the weight of the papal authority behind it.

Just as the contents of Father Raymond's letter had been circulated through and beyond Lyon, so now were the contents of this letter from the cardinal. Bishop de Bruillard remarked somewhat acidly that there was obviously nothing very secret about this letter asking for the secrets. He judged, however, that there might be something to the suggestion that the Holy Father was interested in the secrets. This view was strengthened when, in mid-June 1851, he received from the cardinal a letter saying, "I have been commissioned by His Holiness to send on to him the secrets and nothing else, the secrets pure and simple. I ask you to have someone put this demand to Maximin and Melanie: that they write the secrets and let me have them. The envelopes should not be fastened; I shall put my seal on them and forward them to the Pope. I ask you to direct that the children write out their secrets in the presence of a priest who has your full confidence, in order that we may be sure that no one has influenced them."

It was time, Bishop de Bruillard saw, to lay the secrets before the Holy Father, but he was determined that this should be done directly, and not by way of Lyon. He would act quickly, for the cardinal had sent word that he would be in Grenoble sometime in July. He evidently meant to force the issue. Accordingly, a priest was charged with the task of going to the minor seminary, talking with Maximin, then bringing the boy to the bishop's house so that he might there put his secret on paper.

It had previously been explained to Maximin that the Pope might one day ask to be informed of the secret, and in that case there would be nothing to do but obey. "If the Pope asks you for your secret, you'll be obliged to reveal it to him," he had been told. Then, as he hesitated, "You know that the Pope counts for more than the Blessed Virgin?"

"The Pope counts for more than the Blessed Virgin," Maximin had expostulated. "Listen, if the Pope does his duty as well as possible, he'll be a saint, but never, never will he be the equal of the Blessed Virgin!"

Again, it had been proposed that he write out the secret, seal it in an envelope, and leave the sealed envelope at the chancery office, to be opened and read only after his death. He had smiled at the idea. "But supposing someone should be tempted to open the envelope," he asked. Then, putting his hand on his heart, "The chancery office in which I'll keep it," he said, "is right here."

Someone else had asked him what he would do if the Pope should say to him, "My boy, you shouldn't believe any of this apparition affair."

Maximin replied, "I'd tell him, 'You'll see!'"

Now, all questions based on supposition and unofficially put were a thing of the past; now, it was a case of the bishop's ordering Maximin to disclose the secret to the Pope. "Maximin," said the bishop's envoy, as they sat in the stiffly furnished seminary parlor, "I'm here to talk to you about something important. Will you promise to repeat nothing of what I'm going to say?"

"Yes."

"Do you believe that the Church has the right to examine and pass judgment on all things religious, such as apparitions, visions, and the like?"

"Yes."

"In order to pass judgment on such things, hasn't she the right, and the obligation, to be thoroughly informed of the circumstances surrounding them?"

"Yes."

"Can the Church make a mistake about matters of this sort?"

"No."

"Can the Pope, the Vicar of Christ, make a mistake about them when he speaks in the name of the Church?"

"No."

"Then, if the Pope should require your secret of you, you would tell it to him, wouldn't you?"

"I'm not yet in the presence of the Pope. When I am, I'll see."

"How do you mean, you'll see?"

"I'll see what he says to me and what I'll then say to him."

"If he commands you to tell him your secret, won't you do so?"

"If he commands me, I will tell it to him."

On July 2, he was brought to the bishop's house. The priest accompanying him thought him altogether too blithe and frolicsome as he made his way to this momentous appointment. He bade the boy calm down and recollect himself, so as to be able to write the secret with exactitude, omitting nothing. "There's nothing for me to be upset about," Maximin assured him. "I recall perfectly all that was said to me. You'll see, when we get there I'll dash off the secret, and I won't have to search for words."

Arriving at the bishop's house, he was shown to a room upstairs, seated at a desk on which paper, pen, and ink were laid out, and told to begin. Two priests stood across the room, to see that he was not interfered with and to observe the manner of his performing this task. Whenever they moved about, Maximin shielded the paper from view.

For a few minutes he sat with his head in his hands. Was he casting his mind back to the apparition, or was he praying? He took the pen, dipped it, shook it so that ink splattered on the gleaming floor. He began to write. The pen flew across the page. The boy went at his work more energetically than adroitly, and presently the inkpot was knocked over, sending a black stream over what he had already written. That sheet had to be destroyed, a fresh start had to be made. He was advised to proceed more carefully, for it would be an affront to His Holiness to send him anything sloppily done. He took more pains and time with the second draught. When it was completed, the bishop was notified and came to the room. Maximin asked him how to fold the written page. The bishop showed him. The boy then put the sheet into an envelope which he closed and secured, pressing Bishop de Bruillard's seal into the molten wax. The two priests signed the envelope as witnesses.

This done, Maximin acted like one from whom a long-borne burden is lifted. "I've been set free," he told them at the seminary, "I don't have a secret any more. I'm just like everyone else. I won't have people coming round to pester me for my secret. Now they can go to the Pope and he'll tell them, if he so wishes." He was asked how it happened that, after refusing for years to divulge his secret, he had agreed to send it to the Holy Father. "The rights of the Pope were explained to me," he said, "and I understood that obeying the Pope would not mean disobeying the Blessed Virgin."

It had been relatively easy to persuade Maximin to communicate his secret to the Pope. To get Melanie to inform him of hers was much harder. To her, too, the bishop sent a priest, who went to the convent at Corenc and interviewed her in the chaplain's quarters. "If the Pope should ask for your secret," he began, "you'd tell it to him, wouldn't you?"

"I don't know."

"How's that? You don't know? Do you think the Pope would make the mistake of asking you for something to which he had no right?"

"The Blessed Virgin forbade me to tell it."

"How do you know that it was the Blessed Virgin? The Church alone can determine that, and we're bound to obey the Church."

"If it wasn't the Blessed Virgin, she wouldn't have gone up into the air."

"The devil can do that. Only the Church can distinguish truth from error in these cases. But you will tell the secret to the Pope if he commands you, won't you, Melanie?"

"I'll tell it to him, but to him alone and for him alone." She would not hear of an intermediary, a messenger. With this, she began to weep, and as the vesper bell sounded through the convent and the interview came to an end, she could not properly take leave of the priest because of her inconsolable sobbing.

At a second interview, she said once more, "The Blessed Virgin forbade me to reveal my secret."

"But the Blessed Virgin wishes us to obey the Pope."

"Oh, it isn't the Pope who's demanding my secret; it's other people who have got at him to have him demand it of me." More tears, and a continued refusal to do as she was asked. The superior of the convent was distressed to see the girl distraught and tearful for the rest of the day. That night Melanie's roommate was awakened by cries coming from the other bed. In her sleep,

Melanie was despondently repeating, "My secret is demanded of me. I must tell my secret to the Pope or be separated from the Church!"

Then Father Rousselot came to see her. Him she had known for some time, and she was well aware of his wholly favorable attitude toward the apparition and his kind consideration in dealing with her. A few words from him, and she quietly agreed to deliver her secret to the Pope. But again she insisted that it was for the Pope alone. Father Rousselot said, "When the Pope knows your secret, will it displease you if he makes it known?"

"No," she answered, "that will be his concern, not mine."

When it came to the actual writing out of her secret, Melanie temporized, burst into tears. But after a little while, she agreed to do as she was told. She sat down, took hold of a pen, began to write. Once she looked up to ask the meaning of the word "infallibly." When it had been explained, she said, "Oh, I didn't know that." A little later she asked the spelling and the meaning of "Anti-Christ." And when the paper had been folded, put into an envelope which was then sealed and signed by the witnesses, and taken away from the convent, she grew disturbed and asked to be let go to the bishop's house in Grenoble. She had remembered a date which should have been included for the sake of clarity. She was allowed to visit Grenoble for this purpose. Afterwards, although not nearly so exuberant as Maximin, she expressed herself as being well content with what she had done.

The secrets were in the bishop's hands by July 3. The cardinal had not yet come to Grenoble. To forestall him, Bishop de Bruillard told Father Rousselot and Father Gerin, rector of the Grenoble cathedral, to go at once to Rome with the two manuscripts. These he put into an envelope along with a letter of his own to the Holy Father.

He wrote that he was sending "these two worthy priests to speak to His Holiness of the event of La-Salette and to place in his blessed hands the writings containing the secrets given on the mountain of the apparition, one to Maximin Giraud and the other to Melanie Mathieu, by the lady who appeared to them and ordered that they be disclosed to no one." He continued, "My two envoys are directed to report to me what it shall please Your Holiness to decide concerning the fact of the apparition of the Blessed Virgin. In case of a favorable reply, will the Holy Father deign to approve the Bishop of Grenoble's saying, in an official pronouncement, that this apparition has all the notes of truth, and that the faithful are warranted in believing it genuine?" He also asked that, should there be a favorable reply, the Holy Father agree to the granting of indulgences to those who made the pilgrimage to LaSalette. He concluded by asserting that, whatever the judgment of the Pope should be, he would gladly accept it, quoting the saying, "Once Rome has spoken, the case is closed."

Father Rousselot and Father Gerin left Grenoble on July 6 and reached Rome on July 11. They were informed that His Holiness, Pius IX, would receive them a week later. On July 18 they presented themselves for the audience and were ushered through the great chambers of the Vatican. The Pope's attitude toward them was markedly gracious. They handed him the envelope bearing the bishop's letter and the secrets. Rising from his desk and walking to a window, he opened the inner envelope containing what Maximin had written. He asked, "Am I obliged to keep these secrets to myself?"

"Holy Father," said Father Gerin, "all power is yours, you hold the keys."

The Pope read Maximin's script, smiled, and remarked that here were the candor and simplicity of a child. The priests concluded that Maximin had been entrusted with a message of mercy and consolation. Then the Pope opened Melanie's envelope. No smile now. This secret seemed to be longer and different in import. As he read, the Pope pressed his lips more tightly together and puffed out his cheeks. When finally he spoke, he said, "Calamities threaten France. But she is not the only one to blame. Italy is, too, and Germany and Switzerland and all Europe. It is not without reason that the Church is called militant." Then, touching his breast, "Here you see her captain. I have less to fear from open impiety than from religious indifference and human respect." He assured the envoys that he would study the secrets at greater length later on.

He observed to Father Rousselot that he had had his book on LaSalette examined by the promoter of the faith, Monsignor Frattini. "He has told me that your book is excellent, that he is well pleased with it, that it is instinct with truth." As for the apparition, he said that it seemed to him to have the character of truth. He would reply to Bishop de Bruillard in a way which would make the bishop forget the annoyances caused him by the Cardinal of Lyon.

That these annoyances were continuing, Father Gerin soon found out. He went home after the audience with the Pope, leaving Father Rousselot to make a stay of six weeks more in the Eternal City. Back again in Grenoble, Father Gerin learned that Cardinal de

Bonald had arrived on July 12, the day after the papal audience. With scant regard for the jurisdiction of Bishop de Bruillard in the latter's own diocese, he had ordered that Melanie and Maximin be brought to him. They had come and had sensed his hostility. He had bluntly demanded that they tell him the secrets. They had refused. He had insisted. They had replied that to tell the secrets was forbidden and, in any case, the Pope was now familiar with them, having received them direct, hence there was no need of their being sent a second time. The cardinal had repeated that he held a commission from the Pope. The pair had asked to be shown the Pope's mandate to this effect. The cardinal had not been able to produce such a document. He had dismissed them and quitted Grenoble.

Father Rousselot used his extra time in Rome to good purpose. He called on various dignitaries. Several times he talked with Monsignor Frattini, who told him that he had carefully read all that the vicar general had written about LaSalette and could see no difficulty in the bishop's building a church at the scene of the apparition, as he wished to do, and allowing to be placed in it tokens of thanksgiving for favors wrought by Our Lady of LaSalette. Cardinal Fornari, at one time nuncio in Paris, said that he, too, had read Father Rousselot's writings on LaSalette, and with much pleasure. Cardinal Lambruschini told the priest, "I have known of La-Salette for a long time. As a bishop, I believe in it. As a bishop, I have preached it in my diocese." Father Roubillon, the Jesuit General's assistant for the provinces of France, said that he was profoundly convinced of the truth of the apparition. Others in responsible positions expressed similar sentiments.

More and more gratified as interviews of this tenor multiplied, Father Rousselot anticipated the satisfaction it would give him to communicate his good news to Bishop de Bruillard. On August 22, he was again received by the Holy Father, who made him a gift of a precious rosary and sent his blessing to Melanie and Maximin. He was given to understand that the matter of LaSalette was in the competence of Bishop de Bruillard to handle as prudence indicated. The Pope would say nothing, but the bishop had the right to make whatever pronouncement on the subject the well-established facts warranted. On August 24, Father Rousselot set out for Grenoble.

Bishop de Bruillard felt that he was now justified in drawing up a doctrinal pronouncement concerning the apparition. Maximin and Melanie had stood by their story through five years of gruelling questioning and testing. Persons pre-eminently qualified to judge the matter, including several bishops, had expressed themselves as accepting the authenticity of the event. Pilgrims had come by the tens of thousands, the hundreds of thousands, some from other countries, other continents. Books on LaSalette had been translated into several languages. Claimed cures were innumerable; cures inexplicable save by miracle were many; an improvement in fidelity to the ways of Christian life was plain to see, and remarkable conversions were on record.

True, there had been challenges to the fact of the apparition, and checks in the process of formulating a favorable judgment. There were the brassily publicized activities of Cartellier and Déléon. There was the very trying Ars incident. There was the derogatory interference of the Cardinal of Lyon. But now, in perspective, these could all be seen to have served a good purpose. Once, when the light of LaSalette had appeared to be blotted out by darkness, when it had seemed that opposition and mischance might destroy the credibility of the happening on the mountain, the not always wise Maximin had shown himself piercingly wise, indeed prophetic, in saying, "LaSalette is now like a plant which in winter is covered over with muck and manure, but which, when summer comes, will bloom all the more beautifully for that very reason." It proved even so. The charges by Cartellier and Déléon had not cast the apparition irretrievably into disrepute; rather, the vehemence and persistence of these charges had prompted an unexceptionably rigorous inquiry, and their refutation was so crushing as to prevent their ever again being raised by anyone of good faith. The Ars incident and the consequent intrusion by Cardinal de Bonald had resulted in speedy recourse to Rome, and that, in turn, had elicited a favorable, if understandably discreet, response from the very center of the Church. All the troubles which the bishop had had to face, and which he, in his advanced old age, faced so unflinchingly and handled so sagely, had worked together unto good.

Bishop de Bruillard now asked his colleague and dear friend, Bishop Villecourt of LaRochelle, later to be a cardinal, to assist him in drawing up the doctrinal pronouncement on LaSalette. Bishop Villecourt had long since come to LaSalette to conduct his own inquiry, and afterwards had been forthright in making known his conviction that an apparition had really taken place. He happily agreed to collaborate on the document, and much of it has been attributed to his authorship. It was completed in September, and Bishop de Bruillard signed it on the fifth anniversary of the apparition, September 19, 1851. It was then sent to Rome, for the scrutiny of Cardinal Lambruschini.

While word from him was awaited, a commission of Grenoble priests inspected a copy word by word; a few minor changes were suggested, and to these the bishop readily assented. In October, Cardinal Lambruschini wrote that he had gone over the document, found it cogent and moving, and would advocate only one small alteration, which was made.

It was then printed, and copies were distributed to all the priests in the diocese, with the direction that it be read, in the 600 churches and chapels under Bishop de Bruillard's authority, on November 16. On that morning, people in every quarter of the diocese heard the staidly formal periods through which joy shone. It began thus: "Five years ago we were told of an event most extraordinary and, at first hearing, unbelievable, as having occurred on one of the mountains in our diocese. It was a matter of nothing less than an apparition of the Blessed Virgin, who was said to have been seen by two herders on September 19, 1846. She told them of evils threatening her people, especially because of blasphemy and the profanation of Sunday, and she confided to each a particular secret, forbidding that these be communicated to anyone.

"In spite of the natural candor of the two herders; in spite of the impossibility of collusion by two ignorant children who hardly knew each other; in spite of the constancy and firmness of their witness which has never varied either when confronted by the agents of the law or by thousands of persons who have exhausted every trick to involve them in contradiction or wrest their secrets from them, it has been our duty to refrain for a long time from accepting an event which seemed to us so marvelous.

"Haste on our part would not only have been contrary to the prudence which the great Apostle recommends to a bishop; it would also have served to buttress the prejudices of the enemies of our religion and of a great many Catholics who are Catholics only in name. While a multitude of pious souls warmly welcomed this reputed apparition as a fact, we again and again considered with care all the grounds which could lead us to reject it. Hence we have braved until now the criticisms which we well know have been directed at us by people, with the best of intentions in other respects, who accuse us, perhaps, of indifference or even of stark lack of faith.

"On the other hand, we were strictly obliged not to regard as impossible an event which the Lord (who would dare deny it?) might well have permitted to further His glory, for His arm is not shortened and His power is the same today as in ages past.

"While our episcopal duty imposed on us the necessity of waiting, pondering, fervently begging the light of the Holy Spirit, the number of wonders noised about on all sides was constantly growing. There was word of unusual cures worked in different parts of France and in other places, even countries far away. Sick people in desperate straits, either given up by their doctors as certain to die soon or condemned to long drawn out suffering, have been reported restored to perfect health after invocation of Our Lady of LaSalette and the use, with faith, of the water from a spring at which the Queen of Heaven appeared to the two herders.

"From the very first days, people have spoken to us of this spring. We have been assured that it had never before flowed steadily, but gave water only after snows or heavy rains. It was dry that September 19; thereafter it began to flow and has flowed constantly ever since: marvelous water, if not in its origin, at least in its effects."

The bishop treated other features of LaSalette, one by one, and outlined the process of investigation and discussion carried on at his insistence. He alluded to his consultation with other bishops, their sharing his view that this was indisputably a prodigy, their being convinced that cures of people in their respective dioceses were miraculous, their allowing public preaching about the apparition and the placing of statues of Our Lady of LaSalette in parish churches. Then came the formal declaration:

"Conforming to the principles laid down by Pope Benedict XIV, and following the path traced by him in his immortal work, *On the Beatification and the Canonization of Saints,* Book II, Chapter XXI, Number 12;

"Having read the account written by Father Rousselot, one of our vicars general, and published under the title *The Truth Concerning the Event of LaSalette* (Grenoble, 1848);

"Having also read *New Documents Concerning the Event of LaSalette,* published by the same author in 1850, both of these works invested with our approbation;

"Having heard the discussions, representing different opinions, which took place in our presence in sessions on November 8, 15, 16, 17, 22, 29 and December 6 and 23, 1847;

"Likewise having read or heard what has, since that time, been written or said for or against the Event;

"Considering, in the first place, the impossibility of explaining the fact of LaSalette in any other way than by divine intervention, whether it is looked at in itself, in its circumstances, or in its essentially religious aim;

"Considering, in the second place, that the marvelous consequences of the fact of LaSalette are the witness of God Himself, manifesting Himself by miracles, and that this witness is superior to that of men and their objections;

"Considering that these two grounds, taken separately or, much the more, together, ought to dominate the whole question and deprive of every trace of validity those contrary pretensions or suppositions of which we declare that we are fully aware;

"Considering, finally, that obedience and submission to heaven's warnings can spare us the new chastisements with which we are threatened, while too long resistance can lay us open to evils beyond repair;

"On the express demand of all the members of our venerable chapter of canons and of the overwhelming majority of the priests of our diocese;

"Having invoked afresh the Holy Spirit and the assistance of the Immaculate Virgin;

"We declare the following:

"1. We give judgment that the apparition of the Blessed Virgin to two herders on September 19, 1846, on the mountain of the Alpine chain situated in the parish of LaSalette, in the territory of the archpriest of Corps, bears in itself all the marks of truth, and the faithful have grounds to believe it indubitable and certain.

"2. We believe that this event acquires a further degree of certitude from the immense and spontaneous flocking of the faithful to the scene of the apparition, as well as from the abundance of marvels which have come in the wake of this event and a very great number of which cannot be called in doubt without violating the rules of human testimony.

"3. Therefore, to demonstrate our lively thanks to

God and to the glorious Virgin Mary, we authorize the cult of Our Lady of LaSalette.

"Given at Grenoble September 19, 1851, the fifth anniversary of the famous apparition.

"✠Philibert, Bishop of Grenoble."

This document was carried by the religious press throughout France and soon appeared in various translations: Flemish, English, German, Italian. The *Osservatore Romano* printed it in its entirety and announced that that newspaper's office would receive contributions for the construction of a church at the site of the apparition. For some time, Bishop de Bruillard had been negotiating for the purchase of this property, and on May 1, 1852, he let it be known that building would soon be under way and the cornerstone would be laid on the 25th of that month. Simultaneously, he announced the founding of a community of priests, to be known as the Missionaries of La Salette, who would be assigned to the church and would minister to the pilgrims, preaching, hearing confessions, saying Mass and distributing Communion. "This group of missionaries," he said, "is, as it were, the seal we wish to place on the other works which, by the grace of God, it has been given us to institute. It is, so to speak, the last page of our testament."

The bishop had not intended to be present for the cornerstone-laying on May 25. He dearly wanted to be on hand, but he was now eighty-seven years old and ridden with illness. The long trip from Corps, the chancy ascent of the mountain, would be beyond him. But he had asked his friend, the Bishop of Valence, to preside at the ceremony, and he urged as many of his people as could to attend.

Little urging was needed. The doctrinal pronouncement had been hailed on all sides, and when the date of the cornerstone-laying was announced, thousands began to make plans to be present for it. As the day drew near, Bishop de Bruillard told his household that he must go to LaSalette. His intention was regarded with misgiving by those close to him. The good old man would be prostrated. But his strong will overrode both the opposition of others and his own infirmity. Word was sent to Corps and LaSalette that he was to be expected on May 24.

Corps was carried away with delight. It was going to be host to two bishops. The approach of the stage carrying Bishop de Bruillard set off a demonstration. Cheers went up. The chief of police made a speech of welcome. The priests, however, were anxious. The ride from Grenoble had been long and jerky. The bishop must be fatigued to the point of exhaustion. If he was, he did not show it. The reception pleased him, and the thought of offering Mass in the morning on the spot where our Lady had stood buoyed him up. He said that he would rest for an hour in Father Mélin's house, then proceed to LaSalette. He was leaving the better quarters in Corps for the Bishop of Valence. The humbler hospitality of LaSalette would suffice for himself.

It was dark when he reached LaSalette. He was greeted by cheering mountaineers carrying lighted torches. Never before had their village been blessed by his presence, and they were determined to give him a reception as elaborate and affectionate as they could make it. The bishop charmed them. They knew of his great age. They had not been prepared for his spryness, his snapping eyes, his winning smile. "How gay he is," they said to one another. "He is made young again by this celebration."

His night's sleep was brief. At 5:45 the next morning

he was ready to proceed. He mounted a horse and, accompanied by a crowd of clergy and people, set off. The perils of the ascent seemed to cause him no trepidation. Those who watched him, wondering whether he would ever complete this hazardous trip, shook their heads in astonishment and admiration as the white-haired figure in episcopal regalia was borne higher and higher, along precipices, on narrow paths, past roaring torrents. The destination was reached a little before eight o'clock. The bishop, who had showed no concern during the difficult two-hour journey, showed emotion when first he set foot on ground to him sacred. There were thousands of pilgrims there ahead of him, and they loosed shouts of "Long live the bishop!" The mountains magnified this loud acclaim. The bishop wept.

He vested for Mass, went to the rude altar, offered the Holy Sacrifice with evident feeling, and this was shared by the throng kneeling on the earth, in the open air, with the gigantic peaks all around suggesting might and mystery.

The solemn ceremony was set for nine o'clock. By then, a fine rain had begun to fall. The two bishops paid it no notice as they went about the rites prescribed for the blessing of a cornerstone. There was so much still to be done before the towering church would stand in this lonely place, against this stately horizon. Wielding a trowel, Bishop de Bruillard knew that this was only a beginning. But it was also an ending.

He already had it in mind to resign his see, so that a younger man might take up its burdens. The following year, at 88, he would do so. In retirement, he would live to be 95. What misfortunes, what changes, he had seen in his many decades as a priest. How fast had gone the dizzying, downward spiral away from God and the things of God. How bemused was the world, and how costly was, and would be, its failure to attend to what counted above all. Yet there was always the divine mercy. Here in his own diocese, it had been manifested in a manner grand and poignant. He had had the privilege of determining and proclaiming the fact of our Lady's coming to LaSalette. Perhaps some would think it a privilege not unmixed with trouble, considering all the tortuous complications of the last few years. But these were paltry in comparison with the success which had crowned the investigation, the certainty which had irresistibly thrust its way through the brambles of doubt and objection. Whatever the future held, the fact of the apparition was now beyond cavil. Yes, he, with his age-touched voice, would join the multitude in the singing of the *Magnificat*. But he would also, with a heart rejuvenated, sing his own *Nunc dimittis*, that canticle of the tottering Simeon as he laid eyes on the Cause of our Joy, bearing the Light of the World:

> "Now thou dost dismiss thy servant, O Lord,
>   according to thy word, in peace;
> Because my eyes have seen thy salvation,
>   which thou hast prepared before the face
>   of all peoples."

9

The horse which carried the intrepid Bishop de Bruillard up the mountain that day in May did not carry
him down. By the time the bishop was ready to leave,
the rain had made the ground slippery and the going
even more treacherous than usual. It was decided that
a litter should be fashioned for the aged prelate, and in
it he was carried by several of the sturdiest men of
LaSalette. Despite fatigue, the evil weather, the dan-
gers of the descent, Bishop de Bruillard was still in
high spirits. The great demonstration attending the lay-
ing of the cornerstone had much to do with this, but
there was something else.

On his return to Corps he was to lift the penalties
under which the former pastor there, Father Viollet,
had long lain. As has been noted, this priest had been
Father Mélin's predecessor at St. Peter's, but had
grossly disobeyed and persistently defied the bishop.
In consequence, he had been suspended. He had not
left Corps, but had stayed on to rally a group of die-
hard partisans about him and make trouble for Father
Mélin. For years this unhappy and divisive situation

had persisted. Father Viollet had been adamant; he had said that he would never yield.

Then, at the beginning of May, when Bishop de Bruillard had announced the imminent cornerstone-laying, Father Mélin had urged a churchful of people to pray diligently to our Lady during her month, with a special view to her effecting a complete and enduring union of the parishioners. It was clear that he was tactfully referring to Father Viollet and his few irreconcilables. He said, "Sometimes the fruit of our prayers is hidden from us. At other times, it is God's good pleasure to afford us the consolation of letting us see what our prayers have effected." He hoped that this was to be one of those blessed other times.

The very next day, when he came into church for early Mass, he was surprised to see Father Viollet kneeling, head bowed, in the shadows. Should he speak to him or not? Better to say nothing just now. Father Mélin went toward the front of the church. He heard the other get up, come after him. They met in the silent sacristy. Looking his successor in the eye, Father Viollet said gruffly, "I wish to abandon the position I have been in." He asked that his confession be heard. The following morning he was again in church, and he went up to Communion with the rest of the congregation.

The news of this reconciliation had been promptly sent to the bishop. In Mary's month, in the month of the launching of an Alpine basilica dedicated to her under the title of Our Lady of LaSalette, in the month when the people of Corps were praying to her for an end of rifts and dissension in their parish, this long-desired but seemingly impossible change had been wrought. And now the bishop was to restore the humbly penitent rebel to his priestly functions. Little wonder that, as he went down to Corps on his improvised litter, he radiated delight. "There will be more rejoicing over one sinner who repents, than over ninety-nine souls that are justified and have no need of repentance."

The bishop had with gratification noted that it was increasingly the custom to refer to Our Lady of LaSalette as the Reconciler of Sinners. That was as it should be. It was of sins and sinners that she had spoken to the awed children; of the offense given God by the transgressor; of the necessity of prompt and perfect conversion; of the penalties sure to follow upon obstinacy in sin, and the favors to follow upon its renunciation. Her primary purpose was to turn men from sin. Conversions, therefore, would be the strongest verification of the apparition, and this notable, belated conversion of the errant priest was directly connected with LaSalette. Father Mélin called it the greatest manifestation of grace that had occurred in the parish since he took it over. His thanks, he said, were daily spoken to Our Lady of LaSalette for this signal favor. So were the bishop's.

There were, of course, miracles in the physical order. If it was the special object of Our Lady of LaSalette to work miracles of grace in the hearts and souls of men, those of a more conspicuous sort were not lacking. By 1850, more than 200 miracles through the intercession of Our Lady of LaSalette had been attested.

From the Bishop of Sens, for example, Bishop de Bruillard had had the circumstantial account of the cure of Antoinette Bollenat in 1847. Mlle. Bollenat, living at Avallon in the diocese of Sens, was in the care of Dr. Gagniard, who had taken his medical degree at the University of Paris. This physician testified that the young woman had enjoyed excellent health until the age of twelve. Then, as the result of an accident, she developed stomach trouble. A year later, vomiting began to be a daily event for her. She could not be touched on the abdomen without suffering excruciating pain and fainting. A tumor became evident, at first egg-size, then constantly growing until, according to the doctor, it filled the entire epigastric region. It was hard and thought to be malignant.

Fainting spells became ever more frequent, varying in length from ten minutes to three hours. The slightest contact would bring these on. The patient, unable to eat, taking only a few drops of milk a day and sometimes not retaining even these, grew steadily weaker. Her voice, said Dr. Gagniard, was so feeble, save when she was in delirium, that to hear what she was saying one had to put one's ear close to her lips. Her fever mounted, she was generally in a heavy sweat, her suffering sharpened to indescribable acuteness. On November 19, 1847, Dr. Gagniard, seeing her thus, told her relatives that, after several years attending the young woman, he could do no more, that nothing could help her now, that death was at hand.

About a week before, Antoinette's condition, with death apparently approaching, had prompted a neighbor to get some water of LaSalette, a few drops of which were to be given to the patient daily, and to ask the parish priest to request prayers to Our Lady of LaSalette. Antoinette was aware of this. Dr. Gagniard was aware of it, too, but, unlike Antoinette, he expected nothing from it. He did not see the young woman on November 20, but on November 21 word went round that she had been cured. He heard the story before he returned to the house where Mlle. Bollenat lived with her brother and sister-in-law. He did not believe it.

The story was that on Sunday, November 21, Antoinette was to receive Holy Communion. Getting her ready and straightening out her bed caused her horrible agony. At about half-past one in the afternoon, when her suffering had subsided, she asked for and was given two or three drops of the LaSalette water. At two o'clock she asked for something to eat. The request astonished the friend watching by her bedside, but, to humor the dying woman, a cup of bouillon with a bit of bread in it was brought to her. For more than four years she had not taken anything of the sort. But now she drank the bouillon, and with no apparent bad effect.

At about half past five, alone for a while, she felt much better than she had since the beginning of her illness. She was without pain. Slowly, tentatively she placed a hand on her abdomen. The contact produced no torment such as the least touch had formerly done. She asked that some clothes be brought to her. This mystifying request was granted by the friend, who was about to leave for home. Alone once more, she pushed herself to a sitting position, then swung her legs over the side of the bed. She stood up. She became dizzy. She sat down again, quickly. Her head cleared. Again she stood up. No dizziness now. Her limbs felt light, supple. She put on her clothes. How long was it since she had worn a dress, she wondered as she smoothed the skirt. Gratitude welled up in her. She knelt by the bed, her head upon her outflung arms, and poured out her thanks to Our Lady of LaSalette.

It was then that her busy sister-in-law hurried into the room and made straight for the fireplace. She had to see that the fire was going and the supply of fuel for the night was adequate. So absorbed in her task was she that she did not even glance at the bed. She was startled to hear Mlle. Bollenat ask for her slippers, but, recalling that the patient had been delirious during the last few days, she did not bother to reply. When the request was repeated, she turned around, saw Antoinette on her feet and walking across the room. She screamed. Her husband, in the next room, heard the scream and ran in. Together they stood in stupefaction, looking at the woman they had thought at death's door.

Mlle. Bollenat smiled broadly, took a chair by the fire, and said, "Please get on with supper. I have a very good appetite tonight." Husband and wife looked at each other, amazed, then tearful. The stunned silence gave way to loud talk. What had happened, they wanted to know. Antoinette told them, and again there were exclamations, followed by laughter, and spontaneous thanks to Our Lady of LaSalette. Reminded anew that the former patient was hungry, her sister-in-law rushed to the kitchen. In half an hour the meal was on the table, and nobody had at it with greater zest than Antoinette.

The next day brought a crowd of visitors. Mlle. Bollenat was questioned over and over, and over and over she told the story of yesterday's happenings. But she was not so preoccupied with all the talk that she failed to do justice to the four hearty meals served her.

When Dr. Gagniard heard of the cure, he shook his head impatiently. What nonsense! He knew this case. He knew morbidity when confronted with it. Talk of a cure was balderdash. He would go to see for himself. In the report he later wrote, he said, "When I saw the sick woman up and coming toward me with an air of ineffable well being and remaining on her feet throughout my visit, when I saw her without pain, digesting everything, vomiting nothing, when I forcefully and most carefully put pressure on the abdomen lately so sore, above all when I could detect no sign of the tumor, I had no recourse but to accept plain fact."

The doctor made a formal, detailed report on the case, covering its history minutely and testifying that since November 21, 1847, Mlle. Bollenat had gone about, eaten, and slept as does one in sound health. The Bishop of Sens instituted a canonical inquiry, and on March 4, 1849, it was declared that this unquestionable cure, occurring after invocation of Our Lady of LaSalette, fulfilled all the conditions and bore all the marks of the miraculous and must be pronounced a miracle.

Attestations of other miracles, quite as well established and as striking, had come to Bishop de Bruillard, but he found these scarcely more impressive than the reports he had been getting right along from the pastor at LaSalette. This was the Father Louis Perrin who had taken charge of the parish just after the apparition. Father Louis had an elder brother who was also a priest, Father Jacques-Michel. Neither was robust, but Father Jacques-Michel was the worse off of the two. Ill health had forced him to give up successive posts as seminary professor, curate, and hospital chaplain. He had come to live with Father Louis at LaSalette, hoping that the mountain air and the tranquility of this tiny, remote, humdrum parish would benefit him.

Salubrious the mountain air may have been, but quiet and leisure were unknown in LaSalette after September 19, 1846. The pilgrim swarms all made stops at the small rectory. The priests went up the mountain with group after group. The visitors asked to be led in prayer. Religious services had to be provided. Arrangements had to be made for visiting priests to say Mass; there was a number of these daily. But, in labor required and in hours consumed, nothing compared with the confessions.

At the end of September, 1848, the Perrins informed Bishop de Bruillard that three-quarters of the pilgrims who had come to LaSalette since early spring that year had gone to confession. These people had caught the true spirit of LaSalette. To see the place of the apparition was a privilege, and it was likewise a privilege to drink the water of the miraculous spring. To talk to one or both of the children gave them a feeling of closer contact with the marvelous event of 1846. But the most telling evidence of their grasping the pith of the message spoken in the ravine was their eagerness to receive the sacrament of penance: to avow their sins, renounce them, declare a firm determination to avoid them in future, receive absolution, accept the assigned penance. It was well enough to come as a sightseer; better to come with firm and lively faith; best of all to come with a heart contrite and resolved to cast off sin and advance in holiness.

The burden of these innumerable confessions fell on the two Fathers Perrin. Father Jacques-Michel, the acknowledged invalid, suffered from asthma; his brother the pastor was afflicted with chronic gastritis. But they uttered no complaint. Hour after hour they sat in the roughly carpentered confessionals erected near the spot where the call to penance had been sounded. The sun might beat down brutally, the rain might fall, scythelike winds might cut across the plateau as the day faded. No matter, the two priests stayed at their uncomfortable posts, hearing out all who presented themselves, leaving only when there were no more to be absolved.

If they could be said to have any leisure, they gave it to writing letters. There poured in upon the rude rectory an avalanche of mail. People afar wanted to know about the apparition, wanted water of LaSalette, wanted to report favors received after petition to Our Lady of LaSalette. The Perrin brothers tried to meet every request, to acknowledge every communication. They sent out thousands of letters, denying themselves rest to write by lamplight long after the turning of the night.

Father Jacques-Michel paid the price of the ministry of mercy in 1851. For five years he had worked as few hale men do. Day and night, without a thought of his precarious health, he had done whatever was required in the service of Our Lady of LaSalette. In Lent, 1851, just as he was rejoicing in the fact that the entire parish had made the Holy Year, with the exception of four obdurate men who would not receive the sacraments, he was gravely stricken. It was decided that he should leave LaSalette and return to his family home where he could get the complete rest he needed. The change of scene brought no change in his condition. On Palm Sunday he was anointed and given Viaticum. He died in Easter week, whispering with his thinning breath his longing to see at last her for whom he had toiled by dispensing to thousands the sacrament of reconciliation.

His brother did not remain long after him at La-Salette. Father Louis Perrin's illness grew more parlous; he was no longer equal to the exertions required of the parish priest of a place so ceaselessly beseiged by the devout and by sinners anxious to be rid of the weight of their guilt. He asked the bishop for an appointment elsewhere. This was granted. Three missionaries of LaSalette took up residence on the mountain itself, in a cabin, in May, 1852. They were the first of the scores of LaSalette Fathers who, in the hundred years to follow, would impart heaven's forgiveness to penitential multitudes.

The building of the basilica progressed slowly. This was not for any want or tepidity of interest or enthusiasm. Bishop de Bruillard's successors equaled him in devotion to Our Lady of LaSalette and zeal for the promotion of knowledge of the apparition, pilgrimage to its scene, and due acknowledgment of the honor done the diocese. It was simply that getting materials to the mountain was most difficult. Everything had to be brought for miles, up the steep, rough paths, with the exception of the stone. This came from the mountain itself: its very substance was refashioned to house the living God to whom, in its primitive state, it had for centuries stood witness, and to proclaim the might and clemency of her who had come as both commander and suppliant to her children. All else was transported from Corps on muleback. The basilica itself was to be a spacious, lofty building capable of accommodating 2,500 people; in addition there were to be two hostels for pilgrims. The amount and variety of supplies, therefore, were both vast; the mode of transport was archaic; little wonder that the construction stretched over a period of years.

Donations to pay for it came steadily to those in charge. There were sizable contributions from the rich, but the bulk of the cost was borne by the poor, myriads of whom gave what they could afford, and more, that this monument to our Lady's concern for humankind might rise upon the heights. There was the touching story of seven brothers, all youngsters, who, having heard at Mass an appeal for a collection to further the basilica, wondered how they might contribute. They asked their mother for a few sous. She had none. They talked over the possibilities for making a bit of money, and decided that their best course was to go fishing and try to sell their catch. Into the icy mountain stream they waded. They did not, like Peter, take any fish with a coin in its mouth. But they managed to get a buyer for what they did take, and, on the following Sunday, they proudly put their gift to Our Lady of LaSalette in the collection basket.

As construction proceeded, pilgrims still came in ever greater numbers. Some of the pilgrimages were so dramatic as to evoke wonder even in those long familiar with the manifestations of piety and penance now identified with LaSalette. For example, one evening when most of the visitors had departed and the workmen had quit for the day and the mountain was all but bare of people, a sizable group was sighted making the ascent. Some in it bore banners; all in it were praying together. A pilgrimage, unquestionably. But why arriving at this late hour? An explanation was forthcoming. These were folk from Allemont-en-Oisans. That morning they had gathered in their parish church to assist at Mass—at one o'clock. At two o'clock they had formed ranks and set out on foot for La-Salette. With time out for a little rest and refreshment, they had been walking for sixteen hours. Again, there were the Good Shepherd nuns from Grenoble who, in thanksgiving for a favor obtained through an appeal to Our Lady of LaSalette, walked barefoot all the way from Corps to the mountain top, a journey of many hours. Still again, there was the distinguished gentleman who walked from Paris to LaSalette, the last forty miles barefoot.

Less spectacular evidences of the penitential spirit inspired by LaSalette could be found in the sight of dozens of people kneeling to make their confessions in every corner of the unfinished, unfurnished basilica. In what would be the sacristy, in what would be the vestibule, on the skeletal staircases, priests sat in the open, and to each there moved a long line of men and women unconcerned about having to confess without the shelter of a confessional.

It was often remarked how many men came to LaSalette and there received the sacraments. The numbers of women were hardly unexpected, but that these should be equaled and sometimes surpassed by the numbers of men was cause for comment. One man gave a typical account of his experience at LaSalette. "I accompanied my wife. When we got there, my ideas were very different from hers. She prayed away and received the sacraments. As for me, I firmly decided to do no praying and to keep away from the confessional. I went over the whole place, out of curiosity and also to see what I could find to criticize. I went into the church, but didn't genuflect or take holy water. Later I went toward the spring, but scornfully. I drank a glass of water from it, but only to make sure that it wasn't mineral water. I recognized it as natural water. It had no effect on me. The next day I followed a crowd of pilgrims to the spring. They drank, and so did I. I had hardly got the water down, when I felt oppressed. I was surprised at this. I drank again. Then I went to the church. I knelt down, a thing I never did. At that very moment something I can't describe, a sort of revolution of well being occurred in me. I began to weep for my sins. Half-an-hour later, I was making my confession to the superior of the missionaries. In so doing I was freed of an enormous weight which had been bearing me down. I had gone thirty years and more without receiving the sacraments."

Another man, a journalist, wrote thus of what happened to him at LaSalette. "I had often had occasion to put in my paper articles dealing with the recent wonder at LaSalette, and I determined three years ago to spend my vacation here, but not for enlightenment or to defend the truth. I didn't suppose that there was any truth in the story.

"When I got here, I discovered no superstition, no money-scheme, no deception, none of that slickness everywhere encountered today. Instead of finding weapons to use against the apparition story, I found myself disarmed. I went away very thoughtful. Would you believe it, all that year I couldn't rid myself of the thought of LaSalette. It kept recurring and disturbing me. At last I resolved to come back secretly, to satisfy my conscience, and to see in all seriousness and without making up my mind in advance, just what there was to this thing.

"I assisted at several religious exercises. I even prayed. I was touched, I was stirred up, but I wasn't yet converted. What to do? How to admit that I was abandoning my advanced opinions to become one of those won over to LaSalette?

"I came away more troubled than I was the first time. All that I had read in St. Augustine I now recalled, and I saw with dismay that it was with me as it had been with him: that I believed more than I wanted to believe and, above all, more than I wanted to act upon. Worn out by the struggle that was going on within me, in one of those moments when God shows compassion for our weakness, I resolved to come here a third time and to leave as either victor or vanquished, a practising Christian or an outright opponent—no half-measures, no zigzagging, but straight all the way.

"I came back. I made a retreat. I went to confession.

I was judged worthy to go to Holy Communion. All my perplexities disappeared. As I had given my family and my friends bad example by my indifference and my neglect of religion, I determined to let them know just where I stood . . . Everyone realized that I was no longer what I had been. I am now serving Mass regularly . . . I do it in penitence and in justice to God."

So it was in countless cases. The lapsed, the case-hardened, the cynical, those who regarded themselves as not merely unreligious but irreligious and even anti-religious fell under the sway of a gentle-seeming but inexorable power which broke the hard-packed, stony surface of their souls and there brought to life and to growth a disused if not forgotten faith, a piety dead or dormant, compunction for sin. Where the beautiful lady had wept, there now wept men who had long mocked at religion, who had gone gladly along with the smug materialism of the age, who had indulged every appetite, whim, mood regardless of the laws of God. Where the unearthly light had shone, there now was routed the darkness of ignorance, error, corruption which had made reeking dungeons of souls meant to be temples of the Holy Spirit.

It was probably this influence for conversion in the apparition which a saint like John Bosco had descried, in the saints' almost instinctive way of recognizing the long-range design of providence in this or that event. He had heard of LaSalette while still a young priest, and straightaway undertook to speak of it on every possible occasion. In 1850 he had published a pamphlet of which 30,000 copies were distributed. In it he told the story and dwelt on its meaning. To him it was clear that our Lady asked reform of men's thinking, choosing, living. "Let us so act," he said, "that this will be to us a source of graces and blessings, serving to rouse in us a faith which is vital, a faith which is efficacious, a faith which leads us to do good and avoid evil, that we may be worthy of the divine mercy in time and in eternity."

It was St. John Bosco's practice each evening to gather together for devotions the many poor and friendless boys for whom he provided a home. He would set them to singing a favorite hymn, and then, in a homely, informal way and in language which for directness and impact one might compare with that of Our Lady of LaSalette, would speak to them of some religious topic. Very frequently, at these meetings in the twilight, his subject would be Our Lady of La-Salette. His purpose was twofold: to foster regard for Mary and to impress on the boys the heinousness of the sins to which she had referred during the apparition. So telling were his words that the urchins who listened closely would, as he finished, lustily break out in their best liked hymn, "We are the Sons of Mary."

Another who found inspiration in LaSalette was Blessed Julian Eymard, founder of the Fathers of the Blessed Sacrament. It was on the holy mountain itself that he was mysteriously moved to begin his work for perpetual adoration of Christ in the Blessed Sacrament that reparation might be made for the evils in which so many lives were bogged down. He had been born, early in the century, not far from LaSalette. When, as a Marist Father, he first heard of the apparition, he had at once believed it authentic. Some dozen times he came to the mountain on pilgrimage. He endeavored to spread the devotion and let it be known that favors, including miracles, which he had asked of Our Lady of LaSalette, were granted. The patent evidences of penitence which he witnessed at

LaSalette deeply affected him. What our Lady had said, he once wrote, showed that heaven was gravely displeased because of the prevalence of sin. And here, in the throngs coming great distances at great inconvenience and publicly professing the contrition which our Lady had urged, he perceived the potency of the appeal to reparation. He would, in still another way, further the task of reparation.

Priests less famous than these also recognized the peculiar force of LaSalette in bringing back the strayed. Near Calais, for example, there was a settlement of people for whom religion had ceased to have any pertinence or weight. The place, in a dreary waste of sand dunes, was known as the Barracks, since its tumbledown buildings had once housed a royal garrison. Father Limoisin, a priest of the Arras diocese, had observed the inhabitants' utter lack of concern with religion, their febrile preoccupation with cheap pleasures and, indeed, debauchery. To see them sinking ever farther into infidelity and immorality pained him. He resolved to do something. To reach these people would be hard enough; to reclaim them seemed to some impossible. He dedicated his endeavors to Our Lady of LaSalette, leaving it to her to fructify the soured and barren field.

When he signified that he had come to the Barracks to stay, he was sullenly stared at. Its dwellers wanted nothing to do with a priest; they resented his presence. Only after much searching and persuasion was he able to find a place in which to say Mass. For this he was, ironically, allowed the use of a frowzy dance hall. There he was at first left severely alone. But he had no intention of reciprocating. Repeatedly he went from door to door; where he was not rebuffed he was but coolly received. Yet he persisted. A few people began coming to Mass, then more and more. He announced that every evening he would conduct devotions to Our Lady of LaSalette and wanted their presence. When he gave them their first news of the apparition, most of his auditors were in tears. They could not get enough of the story. It swept through the squalid settlement like a cleansing tidal wave. Conditions changed radically. Fervor replaced dissipation.

Father Limoisin proposed to build a church which would be a center of pilgrimage in honor of Our Lady of LaSalette. The notion was called preposterous. Calais heard of it with incredulity, with laughter. But when the priest invaded the city with no fewer than 200 men from the Barracks, so long of dismal repute, in order to beg funds for the church, ridicule gave way to wonder. Two hundred of those rogues and rakes from the Barracks canvassing for a church? Who could resist?

This resolute man, who attributed all his astounding success to Our Lady of LaSalette, carried through the improbable project. The church rose. A school was built, and then an orphanage, a convent, a rectory. The unwelcome pastor became the hero of a people reformed out of all recognition. And his devotion to Our Lady of LaSalette, taken up by his parishioners, was spread by them with an enthusiasm matching his own. They eagerly co-operated in implementing his plans for a shrine to which those who could not get to southeastern France might come. This pilgrimage was set for the anniversary of the apparition. A preparatory novena was offered from the 10th to the 19th of September each year. It attracted hundreds, then thousands, was graced by conversions, miracles, and the by now characteristic feature of innumerable confessions, to hear which many priests had to be brought in.

Outstanding in the edifying history of LaSalette is the national pilgrimage of 1872. In a few months between late summer of 1870 and the early days of 1871, France had suffered the disaster and rankling humiliation of a quick and relatively easy defeat by Prussia. Then the Commune had raged, with Frenchmen slaughtering Frenchmen while the Prussian army looked on. France supped full on horrors and calamities. The warnings of Our Lady of LaSalette were recalled, and it was suggested that a national pilgrimage of reparation be organized, with all parts of the country represented in a solemn convergence upon the place where those warnings had been voiced.

Thiers, then president of a disorganized, partially destroyed, and all but bankrupt country, said disdainfully, "Pilgrimages are no longer among our customs." But that he did not speak for the people and would be proved wrong by them was shown as the call for a national recourse to LaSalette was everywhere answered. From Paris, Amiens, Rouen (names with the reverberations of history in their very sound), from the port of Calais and the port of Marseilles, from the Loire, from the Marne, from the Seine, from the Rhone, from the lowlands and the highlands, from areas fouled by mines and areas green with vines, they came in a pilgrimage unprecedented, to make supplication for a France which had been in some measure prodigal and had been cast down into the dust. "Save, O, save France," the men and women from every sector pleadingly sang as they crested the mountain and sank to their knees on the blessed ground.

In a way, this marshaling of the people foreshadowed what would happen a few years later when, in 1879, the basilica would at last be consecrated and the statue of Our Lady of LaSalette would, by the Pope's leave, be crowned. Officiating at the consecration was the Cardinal Archbishop of Toulouse, and the coronation was carried out by the Cardinal Archbishop of Paris, acting as papal delegate for this rite. Bishops and archbishops in numbers were on hand, and with them came pilgrims from every diocese, a concourse which, in origin, in dress, in speech was the kaleidoscope of France in miniature, paying homage to her who had so favored their land, making suffrage for the balm of her lenity upon it, upon them.

The LaSalette Fathers, busy with the work of reconciliation where the summons to it had been sounded, received many applications for their society. Eventually they were able to send missionaries far beyond France to carry our Lady's message under skies alien to them but not to her. Some went to Poland, to found a seminary which became a center of pilgrimage where, in accents odd to a French ear, crowds cried aloud their praise of Our Lady of LaSalette and their petitions for pardon. Others went to England, still others came to the United States. Genuine mission territory was entrusted to yet others, in Madagascar and in Burma, and peoples black and yellow learned to know and love and appeal to her who had given more than metaphorical meaning to the phrase "clothed in the sun." Statues representing her appearance to Maximin and Melanie were set up in Rome, in Switzerland, in Spain, in Belgium, in the Pacific Islands, in India. An image of her could be found in a convent garden in Indo-China. A church was dedicated to her in Rio, and that capital named a street after her.

From continent to continent, across the measureless oceans, her renown had winged. But, better and more pleasing to her, her message had gone abroad, to the ends of the earth: the warning to be quit of sin and to turn submissively to God. Maximin and Melanie had obeyed her. Puzzled though they were as to how they could possibly fulfill her order that they bring her words to all the people, they had done what they could. It sufficed. Those words were taken up in La-Salette, in Corps, in Grenoble, and sped on their way around the world.

10

Maximin and Melanie temporarily enjoyed a charismatic privilege, not for their own sake but for the sake of others. Such a privilege is something quite different and distinct from exceptional personal holiness, which these two could never claim. A charismatic gift does not involve or imply exceptional personal holiness.

But some, who ignored this fact, called the whole LaSalette story into question as the adult careers of the two witnesses unfolded. Not that those careers were disreputable. At worst, they were disappointing. Still, there were critics, and not necessarily malicious critics, who maintained that LaSalette came under a cloud when it was fully evident that Maximin and Melanie were not, and would not be, saints. This contention was unreasonable and at odds with what the Church, most notably in the teaching of Benedict XIV, holds. Even had the pair gone on to sanctity of the first order, the authenticity of the apparition would not have been established thereby. Its authenticity could be determined only by examination of its every intrinsic feature. This had been done. It had not been prophesied, promised, or required that Maximin and Melanie should become extraordinarily holy; it had merely been required that they transmit the message.

In 1858, twelve years after the apparition at La-Salette, our Blessed Lady appeared to Bernadette Soubirous at Lourdes, not once but many times. Bernadette entered a convent, remained in that convent, died there in 1879, at 35. In the interval between the Lourdes apparition and her death, Bernadette *became* a saint. This was a gradual, painful process not at all manifest to her sisters in religion. Indeed, many of them thought her the least of their company: this short, common-featured, laconic, shy religious who was subjected to humiliations, reprimands, and insults. The Superior General of the community, who had been Bernadette's novice mistress, said, after the young nun's death, "Bernadette was a good ordinary religious." No more than that.

The Lourdes story did not stand or fall by what Bernadette was subsequently or what people subsequently thought of her. No more did Bernadette become a saint just because of the apparition. "What is most encouraging in Bernadette," writes Father Henri Pettitot, O.P., in his superb book, *The True Story of Saint Bernadette*, "what draws us to love her quite specially, and to invoke her with the greatest confidence, is that throughout her life, and especially during the thirteen years spent in the convent, unaided by revelations, ecstasies, or extraordinary graces, leaning only on the staff of the Cross, she had to climb slowly the way of sorrows to Calvary. It was by that road, and by a death in great suffering, that she reached the Thabor of perfection and canonization."

This point established, it remains to say something of the lives of Maximin and Melanie after 1850, the year when Maximin entered the Grenoble minor seminary, and Melanie became a postulant at the convent of the Sisters of Providence at Corenc.

At the seminary, Maximin was like a wild bird which has been shut up in a cage. He was no student. The discipline sat heavy on him. He thought principally of vacations. His attention was too often set on the next holidays. If only the twenty-eight days until vacation would pass quickly, he once wrote to Sister St. Thecla. To be free of class and the exact, unvarying regime, to be free in the busy streets of Corps or on the inviting mountain paths—this was his consuming desire.

Yet the scholastic routine did not break the spirit of this irrepressible optimist. He always expected to do better than his record would warrant. In one breath he would speak of recourse to St. Joseph to help him just to get by. In the next, he would confide his belief that he might well take a prize. At times he would work furiously, at other times he would laze along.

At the end of his first year as a seminarian, he was taken on vacation to the Grande Chartreuse, of all places. To see this ancient monastery might be entertaining enough, but to make a stay in it, with its austere silence and its conformity to the strictest of rules, was not likely to be recreation for one like Maximin. He was told that a monk had died and that, if he chose, he might assist at the funeral. His curiosity was piqued, but what he saw caused him to shudder. "Fear consumed me," he wrote to Sister St. Thecla. "The way in which the monks are buried, that strikes you with fear! They are buried without any casket. They are fixed to a board and then covered with earth." The reality of death, undisguised, unprettified, made no appeal to the thoughtless, skipping Maximin.

He informed the nun that the food was all right at the monastery, but being so much alone bored him.

"The days seem like months," he said, the more so because it was suggested that he do a bit of work on his Latin and his French. When he left, the prior gave his impressions of Maximin to Father Rousselot: "The boy seems to me to be fundamentally all right and to have good qualities, but he is volatile."

Would he return to the seminary? There was doubt that he would. He went to Grenoble, with some idea of going to work. He lodged in a hostel which the Christian Brothers conducted for the benefit of artisans. He was apprenticed to a mechanic. He lasted two weeks.

In the fall of 1851, he was back in the seminary. Again he was sure he would take honors, again he did nothing of the kind. The following summer he spent as the guest of the pastor at Meyrié, who attempted to tutor him. This priest believed that their work together was not without fruit, and even that he discerned the makings of a student of sorts in Maximin. After the weeks of study, the priest took Maximin on a vacation trip, every bit of which the boy enjoyed, even a session with some Jesuits who lengthily questioned him concerning the apparition and were surprised at the quality of his answers.

Still another year at the seminary saw little progress. It was therefore decided that he should go to a second priestly tutor, this time Father Chambon, the pastor at Seyssins. Father Chambon's kindness and patience were heroic. Maximin stayed with him three years, was always most considerately used but never spared the necessity of working at his studies. There survive some notebooks he kept at this time, the handwriting execrable and the corrections by his teacher numerous and emphatic. In one of them there is a discussion of religion larded with quotations from the Scriptures, the classics, the Fathers of the Church, St. Thomas, Bossuet. Maximin was learning, or at least he was learning to borrow liberally from some manual of apologetics.

During his years with Father Chambon he was taken to Rome. There he spent eight days. His heart was set on meeting the Pope. The sights of the city, the streets and buildings instinct with history, the overwhelming monuments of antiquity, the noble churches, these made little impression on him. He wanted to meet the Pope. To do so, he haunted those thoroughfares where, he was told, Pius IX sometimes made an appearance. He even managed to borrow the uniform of a French soldier when he heard that His Holiness might review a body of French troops. Finally, though his sojourn was so short, he was allowed a private audience. He later jauntily assured his friends that he had been quite at his ease with the Holy Father and that the meeting had gone off very well.

By 1856, it seemed possible for him to enter the major seminary for courses in philosophy and theology. By dint of personal instruction, of repeated drilling, he had been rendered at least not flagrantly unready for this step. Did he want to be a priest? Yes and no. He would like to be a priest on his own conditions, a priest foot-loose in foreign parts, a free-lance missionary. Or again, maybe it would be better to become a soldier performing prodigies of valor in defense of the Pope. He didn't know. He wasn't sure. He remained at the major seminary for something less than two years. When it came to the reception of tonsure, which would make him a cleric set off from the lay state and on the way to minor, then major, orders, he withdrew. This was not the life for him.

What next? A try at college for an arts degree. It ended unsatisfactorily. All right, he would become a doctor. He had seen doctors at work by the bedside of the sick and in hospitals. He would give such service to the ailing. He went to Paris to fit himself for medicine. He soon lowered his sights. Being a doctor was beyond him, but at least he could be a pharmacist. He couldn't, though.

The bootless years in Paris were a limbo of misery. There were his academic failures, so glaring as to be definitive: he just wasn't of professional calibre, he didn't have it in him to learn the basic minimum. In addition, there was the city, vast, impersonal, sophisticated, swift-running. Its temper and tempo were alien to a child of the mountains and their plain, leisurely towns. Paris baffled and wounded him. He could not fit in. The loneliness in the midst of the milling herd was unsupportable. And he was poor. He had no sense of economy, no money-craft; the funds that friends had given him trickled unaccountably away. He held casual, menial jobs for a few days, then was discharged. Often, he was hungry. Often, he spent the interminable night shuffling through deserted streets or trying to get some sleep in a doorway or on a park bench where he was nipped by the wind, chilled by rain or clammy fog. If those who had thought him always elated could see him now, they would observe that his mood was not unchanging. It was almost despondent.

At last, threadbare and exhausted, he left Paris. A marvelous idea had come to him. He would go to Rome and become a papal zouave. He remembered the colorful costume, the self-conscious strut, the aura of importance, the admiring attention given by passersby. Somehow, he was admitted to the ranks of these guards of His Holiness. He ate regularly now, and heartily. But he proved no soldier. In six months he resigned; his resignation was gratefully received. There is extant a picture of him in the zouave's regalia. Short, plump, sad-eyed, he looks anything but lean, muscular, and militarily smart. The oriental uniform accentuates his stoutness, the cummerbund merely draws attention to his bulging waist. His hands are pudgy. He is double-chinned, round-faced. The luxuriant moustache looks like a theatrical device gummed to the upper lip of a beardless child.

Back in France, he impulsively lent himself to a harebrained enterprise of which detractors of LaSalette made much. He was prevailed on to endorse a liqueur called "Salettine." Garish posters advertising it and saying that "the herder of LaSalette" recommended it were stuck up all over Grenoble. The venture quickly failed, but not before Maximin, who had been imposed on because he badly needed some money and saw nothing unfitting in what he did, regretted his association with it.

When France declared war on Prussia in 1870, he was called to the colors. He never went into battle, but spent the time of his service in barracks in Grenoble. He was now thirty-five years old and in poor health. Like his father, he was an asthmatic, and his neglect of himself, especially during the wretched years in Paris, had aggravated his congenital weakness. After the defeat of France, he went back to Corps, and there he passed the brief remainder of his life.

He died in 1875, at the age of forty. He set out for eternity from the same little house from which he had set out, twenty-nine years earlier, for the job with Pierre Selme that was to be the occasion of his first and unprepared for encounter with eternity. In his last days he had gone more than once to the scene of that encounter, and he never tired of describing the apparition for whoever would hear him. He knew that his life was guttering out, received the sacraments fervently, took daily some of the water of LaSalette. On March 1, death claimed him. He was buried in Corps, but at his express and earnest request, his heart was placed in the basilica on the mountain.

He had no money, a few shabby effects. But he had drawn up a testament which left all that he had to give: reaffirmation of his longtime witness to the apparition.

"In the name of the Father and of the Son and of the Holy Spirit. Amen," it read. "I believe in all that the holy, apostolic, Roman Church teaches, in everything defined by our Holy Father, the Pope, the august and infallible Pius IX. I firmly believe, even were it to cost the shedding of my blood, in the renowned apparition of the Blessed Virgin on the holy mountain of La-Salette, September 19, 1846, the apparition to which I have testified in words, in writings, and in suffering. After my death let no one assert that he has heard me make any retraction concerning the great event of La-Salette, for in lying to the world he would be lying in his own breast. With these sentiments, I give my heart to Our Lady of LaSalette."

All very touching, said the captious, but one must not be diverted from the stubborn fact that Maximin's life was shockingly at odds with the role which he had claimed for himself: the bearer of a message from Mary to men. That life did not accord with what one has a right to expect from a person so signally favored.

Was this true?

Looking over the years from 1846 to 1875, one must conclude that Maximin was unstable. It is hard to keep straight the sequence of his moves from place to place, pursuit to pursuit. He was at the Sisters' school for a while, in and out of seminaries minor and major, living with one tutor then another, traveling, trying his hand as a mechanic, as a college student, as a candidate for a doctor's diploma or a pharmacist's license, doing odd jobs in Paris to ward off starvation, serving a few months as a papal zouave, letting his name be used in the promotion of a liqueur. Obviously, this is not a record evidencing steadiness and consistency. What was behind its vagaries?

In the first place, there was Maximin's background. His father was the very reverse of dependable. Of regularity and application he gave the boy no example. He was a drifter, a spendthrift, a seeker after pleasure and oblivion, irrationally expecting that sometime, somehow, he would have a stroke of good fortune without lifting a finger. In his formative years, this is what his one surviving parent held up for his imitation. Maximin did not know a mother's interest and care. Moreover, he was unwelcome at the family hearth. He was never checked on, consistently and constructively corrected. So long as he kept out of the way, he might do as he pleased, whiling away the daylight hours, and had only to fear the cuffing and cursing which some errant offense would set off. Of training in right habits he had none. In fact, the wonder is that he was as good as he was, that he did not fall into delinquency and perhaps even depravity, that he remained simple and innocent.

In the second place, Maximin was violently uprooted. Until September, 1846, he had known only the uncalendared existence of a street arab in Corps, and, in the natural way of things, there was no likelihood that his condition would change. He would grow up physically, he would age chronologically, but he would, in all probability, remain an indolent lounger at street corners or possibly in cafés. Then came the term of employment by Selme and, during it, the apparition. He suddenly was transformed into a figure of consequence. He had to go to school. He had to go to school far beyond the period expected of, or possible for, all but a handful of his contemporaries in Corps. He must aim at becoming in his adult life something important. What? Well, say, a priest.

Did Maximin have a vocation? No. That fact, in time, became indisputable. But it was not so from the start. He had to be sequestered and sheltered for his own good. Let him try the seminary. Candidates less promising than he had made exemplary priests. He was not intellectually gifted, but could anyone in that place and period be unmindful of the history of the Curé of Ars? No one tried to force Maximin to be a priest. He found the seminary not wholly disagreeable, and spoke now and again of a wish to be a priest. But when a fixed decision could no longer be postponed, when it came to entering the clerical state, he stepped back. The priesthood was not for him. In this, he was honest and honorable.

Could he then go back to the life in Corps he had dropped more than a decade before? Impossible. His father was dead; there was no household to receive him. Besides, the years had given him a taste for the world beyond Corps. He had traveled; he was educated, or at least he had long been in school. He must amount to something. But he was prepared for nothing. His schooling had been channeled toward the priesthood; it was narrowly specialized. And no one was going to expend on him, for another line, all the effort that had gone into his coaching in seminary subjects. He was without aptitudes, skills. He was like his father in believing that he could be almost anything he chose. He differed from his father in being put to the disillusioning test. He was fit only for the pressureless, uncomplex, uncompetitive countryside. But from that he had been divorced by a succession of events. It was only in the closing days of his life that, whether through wisdom or happy chance, he went back to his beginnings, and it was only when he went back to his beginnings that he recaptured the little contentment that was ever to fall to him in the natural order.

Was it not cruel, this uprooting and the price it entailed? At first glance, yes. But Maximin had been chosen as a witness. "Martyr" and "witness" are the same word. No one will suggest that, in the classical sense, Maximin was a martyr; he was not even a saint. But he was a witness, an appointed witness, and his witness brought him pain. The pain was not of his election. For a long time he did not accept it. But in the end he saw that it was part of the pattern; then he did accept it. Homeless and itinerant, he spoke everywhere of the apparition, in his journeys in Italy, his stays in one or another part of France. He made known to as many people as he met what he had seen and heard at LaSalette.

He was a witness in another way: in his faithful and tender, if never esoteric, devotion to our Lady. In his up-and-down days as a student he edified one of his priest-tutors by his request that they say the full fifteen decades of the Rosary together at night. In his days of doomed effort to measure up as a papal zouave he edified a fellow aspirant by his observance of our Lady's month. In his down-and-out days in Paris he edified strangers by his regular visits, in tattered clothes and broken shoes, to the shrine of our Lady in St. Sulpice. He was undoubtedly hers.

Why, then, did she not do more for him? To advert

again to Bernadette, what did our Lady do for her? The shelter of the cloister was thrown about her, yes: but only that she might go the Way of the Cross in seclusion. Maximin's was an unwalled and wandering Way of the Cross, drawn out and without comforting. The predilection of the Mother of Sorrows is discerned in sorrows. He had no reproach to address to her. At the last he grieved that she might have something for which to reproach him. He said that the apparition had done much for him. It had put him in the way of getting a good Christian education, opening to him a whole universe of basic reality of which he had known nothing. Our Lady, he said, saw to it that he was placed in the company and custody of holy priests, that he was led on to goodness, protected from the evil which kills the soul. Had he not seen her, he told an inquirer, he would almost certainly have gone far from God, into the dread morass of iniquity.

But had he, in fact, been guided away from the swamps? Wasn't it true that he drank to excess and was named a drunkard? He had been seen tipsy, and this was enough for some people to stigmatize him as a sot. Were he a heavy drinker, it would not be wholly unexpected. Wasn't he the son of Giraud who spent most of his time in liquor and had taught his tiny son, still dwarfed by the bar, to drink? But Maximin did not go his father's way. One of his fellows in the papal zouaves who discovered his identity and thereafter observed him closely, wrote to his own father that a single glass of poor wine was enough to befuddle Maximin. Although this young man did not know the word "allergy," he shrewdly suspected that Maximin was one of those persons whom even the smallest quantity of alcoholic drink affects strongly and patently. There was the substance of it: a glass of wine, in countries where wine was invariably part of one's meal, and Maximin was for a time addled and thick of tongue. This is something other than addiction to drink. Had the latter been Maximin's habit, he probably would have sickened, collapsed, and died in his twenties.

This same fellow zouave observed to his father that Maximin had a distaste for jokes even slightly off-color. The racy talk of soldiers was not for him. He never indulged in it, and, when he chanced to overhear it, it palpably disgusted him. "His heart remained always worthy of the Blessed Virgin," said his friend, "and was never soiled." The same thing was remarked by associates during his years in Paris. When other students suggested picking up street-walkers, Maximin was horrified. He never got away from poverty and a humble station; no more did he ever get away from his childhood purity.

The more one considers Maximin, the more impressive is he. "Our Lady left me as I was," he replied to someone who had said that, having beheld her, he should have thereafter been unlike the general run of mortals. Perfection, in any dramatic form, he did not attain. But he was true to his mission, and he demonstrated that wretchedness does not inevitably lead to immorality and irreligion. In the midst of failure, homelessness, want, suffering, he was mindful of God, trustful in our Lady, proof against formidable temptation. Thus, he was a living refutation of the easy assumption, current in his day and in ours, that material conditions determine whether people will adhere to virtue or to vice, that sin is to be expected and explained away when security and plenty are lacking. Heaven would not hear of this fallacy. Maximin was chosen to announce the truth that sin leads to misery and must be expiated if there is to be order on earth and well being among men. He was chosen, too, to announce heaven's unfailing concern for mankind entangled and tormented in the web of its own folly. A failure by worldly standards, he did not fail her who had chosen him.

11

Melanie, the older of the two herders, outlived Maximin by many years. Fourteen at the time of the apparition, she reached the age of seventy-two. Her adult life, spent in preoccupation with religion, might at first sight appear seemlier than his. Actually, it thrusts greater problems on the defender of LaSalette. But these problems can be settled without detriment to the apparition and, indeed, serve only to reinforce its authenticity.

Melanie was eighteen when she entered the novitiate of the Sisters of Providence at Corenc in 1850. She was at the novitiate almost four years, but never became a professed religious. Bishop Ginoulhiac, who succeeded Bishop de Bruillard in the see of Grenoble in 1853 and was as firmly convinced of the truth of LaSalette, forbade it. The reason was Melanie's refusal to obey his order that she cease speaking of spiritual favors and powers of prophecy with which she claimed to be endowed, and address herself to the essential and exacting task of becoming an inconspicuous and disciplined nun. What had happened after the apparition had rendered Melanie incapable of this.

179

Prior to September 19, 1846, she had been ignored, left to herself, counted as nothing. Practically from the morrow of infancy she had had to work as a slavey, and so long as she did the assigned labor she got no notice. Her life had been solitary. She was, so far as others were concerned, a cipher.

Then, suddenly, it seemed that the whole world was looking at her, with gimlet-eyed intensity, with extreme deference. From 1846 to 1850, pilgrims innumerable were always asking to see her. Granted the coveted privilege, they gazed on her with wonder and respect. To have a word with her was a prize for which they contended. Bishops called at the convent in Corps to interview her; so did government officials, high officers in the army, men and women bearing illustrious names, ancient titles.

At the beginning of her new status she disliked this attention amounting almost to religious homage. But, getting used to it, she came to enjoy it, to require it. Sister St. Thecla, as has been noted earlier, was troubled by fear that the girl's head would be turned. But any apprehension on that score could, it was supposed, be put aside when Melanie announced her intention of becoming a Sister of Providence. That would mean leaving Corps and going to Corenc, where her celebrity would cease and the curious could not pursue her, where she would conform to a leveling rule.

Had she disappeared, at Corenc, into the anonymous round of the novitiate, all might have been well. But a capital mistake was made; on whose responsibility it is hard to say. Even at Corenc, pilgrims to LaSalette were permitted to see her almost at will. They treated her with reverence, which was exaggerated and bordered on the absurd. A priest recorded that he saw Melanie in the convent parlor at Corenc surrounded by priests who wrote down everything she said, as if she were an oracle. He spoke to one of them who, he noticed, had already filled three pages with jottings of Melanie's talk. "Father, what are you doing?" "I am writing down everything she says because it is most edifying. I'll read it next Sunday from the pulpit to my parishioners."

Melanie heard this and made no protest. By now she had evidently come to think of it as nothing out of the way, as only her due. This complacency was a great change from the abrupt, embarrassed rejection of flattery which had once been characteristic of her. Long exposure had had its effect.

She was in need of retirement and quiet, of instruction and direction in the principles and practices of the spiritual life, the religious life. Instead, the poor creature was on exhibition, an object of profound and one might say almost superstitious regard, and her every word was snatched up as if it were divinely inspired. Increasingly she took satisfaction in the part expected of her and endeavored to play it to the hilt. To be out of the spotlight, once her wish, had now become intolerable for her. And when Bishop Ginoulhiac, shortly after taking office, directed that Melanie be treated like any other novice and that her public appearances cease, she resented it. Her references to him in later years show that this resentment underlay much of her peculiar conduct. Her chance to settle down to a simple, hidden life in religion had been destroyed by the foolish exceptions made in her favor. She now craved to be heard as an enunciator of the divine will. Her unbridled singularity made it impossible that she remain at Corenc.

In January, 1854, the bishop suggested that she go for a while to the Daughters of Charity at Vienne. She was with them but briefly, for her failure to obey and her more and more imperious self-will led to clashes with the superior, a display of something like hysteria on Melanie's part, and disorder in the house. She was allowed to go to the convent at Corps, a dubious move since it brought her into the midst of the LaSalette pilgrimages once again and led her to assert herself in a fantastic way.

In September of that year she went to England, to reside at the Carmelite convent in Darlington. She applied for acceptance by this community and was given the Carmelite habit in February, 1855. It cannot be determined whether or not she had a vocation to the Carmelite life. But it can be said that the circumstances of her reception were unfortunate. The event, which should have been given no publicity, was surrounded with resounding publicity. The press identified her, announced the place and the hour of her entering upon her new venture in the religious life, and the ceremony consequently drew many people. This was the very reverse of what Melanie now needed. Nonetheless, it seemed for a while that she might have found her place and her peace behind the Carmelite grille. But in 1860 she left the Darlington convent, after disagreements and disturbances, and returned to France.

She made yet another attempt to become a nun, this time with the Sisters of the Compassion, a new community which at first took her in as a guest and later, after she had been released from her vows as a Carmelite, permitted her to wear their habit. When the Archbishop of Corfu, in the Ionian Islands off the west coast of Greece, asked the Sisters of the Compassion to send two nuns to take charge of an orphanage in Cephalonia, Melanie was one of those appointed to the post. But she was soon back in France and no longer associated with the Sisters of the Compassion.

Next, she once more tried Carmel, withdrew; once more tried the Sisters of the Compassion, withdrew. For some years she led a wandering life, refused by religious houses which she attempted to enter. The Bishop of Castellmare, in Italy, befriended her, and provided her a home in his diocese for some seventeen years. But her travels were not over. She lived for short periods here and there in France, visiting LaSalette at least twice. Now she was in France, now in Italy, never for very long in either. It was in Italy, at Altamura, that she spent the last months of her life.

In the town she had a rented room. Each morning she was at the cathedral for early Mass, an old woman in a black dress and an outmoded black bonnet. Her regular attendance at the same Mass made her a familiar figure to the rest of the congregation. When, on December 15, 1904, she was missing from her accustomed place before the altar, some of the people went to the house where she boarded to see whether she was all right. The door to her room was locked. Loud knocking, repeated calls brought no response. The door was forced. There, stretched on the floor, dressed for her walk to Mass, Melanie lay dead.

Had she died earlier, for example in her days at the convent school in Corps when she expressed a wish to leave the ugly earth, she would have been spared much pain and distress, and the cause of LaSalette would have been spared the impediments of her making in her mature years. But, as in the case of Maximin, the very things about Melanie which create difficulties are seen, on closer analysis, to buttress the cause of La-Salette.

Melanie's career is explicable in much the same way

as Maximin's: it is in some part accounted for by her pathetic background. Yet, where in Maximin we have to complain of instability, in Melanie it is rather stubbornness that we must deplore. He moved about from one spot to another, from one occupation to another, and sometimes showed evidence of frivolity. He gave the major seminary, the immediate avenue to the priesthood, a single try, then, convinced of his unsuitability, stepped out of it and never sought to return to it. Melanie, on the other hand, made a number of attempts to become a religious, was never convinced that she did not have the capacity and even the right to be admitted to profession, and each time left feeling sure that she was right and everyone else, especially the superiors she declined to obey, was wrong. Of course she was wrong.

But how much can she be blamed? It was to her credit that she held fast to the facts of the apparition, despite repeated and nagging inquiries, despite threats and troubles of no light nature. Her tenacity in this was brave, gallant, admirable. It should have been recognized that this very tenacity might, in other connections, have unfavorable consequences were she not handled in just the proper way. To say it still again, her subjection to the public view at Corps and at Corenc was the worst thing that could have happened to her. It incited pride, it confirmed her in a sense of innate importance and autonomous authority. What she was to do amiss in the decades ahead is obviously attributable to the feeling of superiority then developed.

Thus, she was one day to write, by herself or in collaboration with someone else, an autobiography in part demonstrably fictional. In it, she told of extraordinary piety and mystical experience in her childhood. These claims were utter nonsense, as the testimony of those who knew her intimately in her first years (testimony gathered shortly after the apparition) and her own earlier accounts of her childhood, incontestably proved. Far from being pious, she had been practically a stranger to religion, and of mystical experience she had none. But she had to contrive a record which would fit the position conferred on her by the gaping multitudes and the lamentably imprudent clergy. She had to establish that she was more than worthy of the regard they gave her and had reason for her singularity. When, in her journeyings from place to place, she was desolate and in fear of disgrace, she had to do something to win back the attention which had become indispensable to her. Hence, the fable of sanctity from the beginning and the awkwardly concocted yarns about visions and ecstasies.

The same appetite for attention in the course of difficulties which some might find discreditable probably accounts for her revelation of what she contended was her secret. This had its inception while she was at the novitiate and the bishop's efforts to keep her within the normal bounds of life there chafed her. To her associates in religion she would mention a set of initials and then say tantalizingly that, could they riddle that, they might have a key to her secret. Such tricks certainly served to keep interest focussed on her. Later, in the roving years, she would disclose what purported to be bits and pieces of her secret. These were of sensational import, and usually had to do with enormities of which priests and religious were said to be guilty and which would provoke spectacular, calamitous requital. Whether or not Melanie was actually making known what she had been told at LaSalette, at least it is plain that the alleged revelations would draw people's notice back to her. It must further be observed that what she said served as a means of venting her grievances against priests and religious whom she held responsible for her vagrant existence in that they had not, as she thought they should have, bowed to the conditions on which she had wanted to pursue a career in religion.

These aberrations of Melanie's have been for some the impassable stone of stumbling in the way of acceptance of LaSalette. Anyone inclined to stop short with them should consider the matter more carefully. In point of fact, they strengthen the case for LaSalette. Melanie's doleful mistakes may have been providential.

In fabricating a childhood history at variance with the actuality, in professing to publish what had been entrusted to her as a secret not to be communicated to anyone, she showed herself frail, fickle, all too human. Yet, this same otherwise undependable person never, for fifty-eight years, changed an iota of her original account of the apparition. All her vicissitudes, all her moods, all her inclination to shift to suit her convenience, all her intense and ungovernable subjectiveness, all her insistence on magnifying herself at whatever cost, did not, as long as she lived, induce her to alter by a syllable the story she had told that first night in Pra's kitchen. This was the one constant in her life, a fixed star over a restless and sometimes tempestuous seascape. The contrast only emphasized the validity of the story. Here, one was forced to say, was something real, objective, something not of Melanie's making.

We have spoken of Maximin's sufferings. Melanie's should not be overlooked. One is quicker to discern, and sympathize with, the sufferings of a humble person like Maximin than with those of a person as self-righteous, self-assertive, and overbearing as Melanie became. But Melanie's sufferings were of a more subtle and excruciating sort than his. It may appear otherwise. Where his health, as he came into middle life, was poor, hers seems to have grown more robust with the passage of the years. She survived into old age, and there is no indication that she was chronically or painfully unwell. She was as homeless as he, in that she went from one town to another, never settling down for long. But wherever she went she was, almost to the last, treated as an honored guest and never without comfortable sustenance, companionship, and even ardent advocates of her most preposterous imaginings. There is nothing in her career like the abject Paris interlude in Maximin's.

But what of her mental sufferings, for more than half a century? Maximin experienced unhappiness; he endured disappointment after disappointment. But his was a resilient spirit. He had ultimately to face his inadequacy, to come to terms with it, and this caused him heartache. And over the closing years of his life, from the forlorn years in Paris until the end, there was a pall of sadness. But in all this there is nothing to compare with the unremitting psychological agitation, the anguish, the torment which Melanie had to bear. Say that she became abnormal; say even that she became neurotic. Does this in any way lessen the fact and the terrible exactions of her inner affliction? She was not responsible for the peculiarities of thought and judgment which mushroomed as she aged. Had she been more sagaciously and resolutely handled by those who had her in charge in her youth, these might have been corrected, or at least contained. They were not, and they tortured her. Hers, then, was a cross less obvious but more cruelly racking than Maximin's, and she is a figure much more pitiable than he. Current knowledge of mental disturbance and its rigors should make this clear to us as it may not have been clear to those whose lives coincided with Melanie's.

She was, on September 19, 1846, briefly caught up, without foreknowledge or choice, into the world beyond the world, and, though she faithfully did what was demanded of her on that occasion, she was reluctant thereafter to remain patiently in the realm of shadows but, in the absence of apt direction, became an eccentric. She was a victim, and her sacrifice should not be despised nor should it be misread as a scandal.

Bernadette was more fortunate than Melanie. It is hardly fanciful to say that, for this, Bernadette owed something to Melanie. By the time that the apparitions at Lourdes occurred, Melanie had already embarked on her incongruous course. By 1858, she had been in and out of the Corenc novitiate, in and out of the house of the Daughters of Charity, and was shortly to leave the Carmelite convent in England. She was already an object lesson in how not to manage an unlettered child who had been used as a messenger by our Lady. The lesson was not lost on those who had the care of Bernadette and the event, in her case, was far different from that in Melanie's.

Melanie's history is a powerful argument for the necessity of submitting all revelations to the judgment and the control of the Church. The Church is the divinely appointed interpreter of them, and those to whom they are entrusted are meant to conform implicitly to her authority both as to what has been communicated to them and as to what they will themselves do or not do. The Church, as St. Thomas puts it, is a permanent charisma which alone can pass on those charismata which, like that granted the children at La-Salette, are but temporary.

The Church, through the bishops of Grenoble, vouches for LaSalette. Successive Popes have often and eloquently encouraged devotion to Our Lady of LaSalette and enriched it with indulgences. The deficiencies and idiosyncracies of Maximin and Melanie are but gargoyles on the monumental, enduring fact of LaSalette.

12

The apparition at LaSalette occurred more than one hundred years ago. Reading of it, we are struck by the many quaint, archaic things in the story: the dress of the two witnesses, the stage coaches, the oil lamps, the immediacy of the Napoleons. We have gone far beyond all these things. Have we gone far beyond the relevancy of LaSalette?

Is it for us of no more than historical interest? Are we to draw from it no more than edification at the resultant conversions, a feeling of awe at the fulfillment of the predictions of famine and unusual illness because the warnings were not sufficiently heeded?

Is it enough that we add devotion to Our Lady of LaSalette to our long-standing devotion to our Lady under other titles?

Or is there anything here of peculiar and pressing pertinence to our own day, our own situation?

Today, as a century back, the alpine shrine attracts hosts of pilgrims in steady flow. True, it is not now visited by so many as travel to Lourdes. But Lourdes is far more accessible than LaSalette. Do the tens of thousands each year who make the strenuous ascent to the place where three weathered statuary groups commemorate the three phases of the apparition do so only out of curiosity or general piety or a longing for favors? Or does LaSalette speak to something in human nature which does not change with the centuries, does it say something of special point and special pith to our age?

The light that shone in the small ravine over which the gigantic peaks stand as if transfixed is still incomparably brighter than the flash attending an atomic explosion. The few words there spoken to two children are still incomparably more timely and apposite (as things eternal always are) than the cataracts of words poured out hourly over radio and television to millions of listeners. One century, ten centuries, cannot stale LaSalette, because its essence is something which has been central to Christian teaching for twenty centuries, and which will never be outworn. What is that?

That our sin, the seed, the matrix, of all our ills individually and socially was agonizingly expiated on Calvary by the incarnate Son of God.

That Mary, just as she was the Mother not simply of Someone called Jesus Christ, but the Mother of Jesus Christ as Atoner, Redeemer, just as she had an active, leading part in the Incarnation, also had an active, leading part in the Redemption, and forever has an active, leading part in the drama of our destiny, in the economy of salvation.

That in heaven she always makes intercession for us, calling upon God to spare us the dread consequences of our wrongdoing and inundate us with the graces we need if we are to turn away from evil and grow in the goodness which is embryonic glory.

That she has her solicitous eye upon each of us, as she did on the insignificant Maximin walking the road that goes from Coin to Corps, and strives mightily to get each of us to walk the road that goes from earth to heaven.

That she constantly calls us to the repentance which is the necessary condition of our admission to the Father's house, in the very same way that the prodigal son's repentance (breaking with his dissolute past, turning his face homeward) was the necessary condition of his admission to his father's house.

LaSalette, then, applies to every age, to everyone in every age.

But there are two features of it most applicable to our own.

The first is its stress on the re-Christianizing of society. Consider what Mary said at LaSalette, and you will see that it constitutes an indictment not merely of individuals but of the whole community of men. The blasphemy, the impiety, the lapse from prayer and mortification complained of are laid to the generality of men. *All* the people are summoned away from these, and to the virtues against which these offend. Society had to a certain extent abandoned God in 1846; society was forcefully told to return to God under penalty of disaster.

In the intervening century, the process of secularization has advanced, in length, in width, in depth, at a rate and to a degree which even the secularists of the middle of the nineteenth century would find incredible. Over vast areas of the earth there tyrannize monsters whose object is the absolute rule of atheism and materialism. In other places, still nominally Christian, a philosophy of life as barbaric in underlying principle, if less ruthless in avowed aim and in methods, obtains. In the former, society is marshaled to war on God; in the latter, society is conditioned to ignore God. In both, the appalling consequences of godlessness are daily more evident. Upon the wasteland the tears of Our Lady of LaSalette are falling; through the wilderness is heard the voice crying from the mountaintop.

The second is LaSalette's stress on mercy. We pride ourselves that this is a humanitarian age, *the* humanitarian age with which no other can compare. But look out across the world and see the ravages of brutality unprecedented. What is our reaction to the sickening sight? *Pity.*

Pity may prove that we have tender sensibilities. It does not prove that we think and will aright. Pity is a matter of feeling, emotion, no more. It can be a disease; it is never a cure. It is far surpassed by *mercy,* which is an attribute of God, as pity is not and cannot be.

Mary, speaking in God's name at LaSalette, manifested mercy: the concern that men renounce their sins, avail themselves of divine pardon, and then proceed in righteousness and peace. Her weeping was prompted by mercy: recognition of man's basic need to know, love, and serve God, recognition of man's increasing failure to do so, recognition of the calamity inevitable in the train of this failure, and a determination to take extraordinary means to awaken man to his error and his peril, lest he perish. In her mercy, she demanded that what was wrong be righted; in her mercy, she pledged that, should this condition be met, all would be well.

Pity prescribes nothing, heals nothing. Mercy prescribes strong medicine, a regimen salutary in the sense of effecting salvation here and hereafter.

The merciful Mother of LaSalette wears on her breast the image of Christ crucified. To one side of it is a hammer. The hammer, wielded by sin, drove in the nails which fixed His hands and feet to the cross. To the other side of it is a pair of pliers. The pliers, wielded by contrite and faithful love, can draw out the nails. Let all who used the hammer (and who is excepted?) now use the pliers.

33 L

Acknowledgements

A number of French works on LaSalette were read as part of the preparation for this book. Those of which principal use were made are:

LaSalette: Précis Historique by E. Picard, M.S. (Villeurbanne, 1946)

La Grace de LaSalette by J. Jaouen, M.S. (Paris, 1946)

Histoire Séculaire de LaSalette by Victor Hostachy, M.S. (Grenoble, 1946)

Les Miracles de LaSalette by Joseph Giray (Grenoble, 1921)

Marie Corédemptrice (Lyon, 1946)

The quotation on page 166 is from *The True Story of Saint Bernadette* by Father Henri Pettitot, O.P., Newman Press, Westminster, Md.

OTHER IMAGE BOOKS

OUR LADY OF FATIMA – William Thomas Walsh (D1) – 95¢

THE SPIRIT OF CATHOLICISM – Karl Adam (D2) – 95¢

DAMIEN THE LEPER – John Farrow (D3) – 85¢

MR. BLUE – Myles Connolly. Modern classic about a contemporary St. Francis (D5) – 75¢

THE CHURCH SPEAKS TO THE MODERN WORLD – Edited by Étienne Gilson. Social teachings of Leo XIII. An Image Original (D7) – $1.25

PEACE OF SOUL – Fulton J. Sheen (D8) – 95¢

LIFT UP YOUR HEART – Fulton J. Sheen (D9) – 95¢

THE PERFECT JOY OF ST. FRANCIS – Felix Timmermans. Novel based on the saint's life (D11) – 95¢

SAINTS FOR OUR TIMES – Theodore Maynard. Eighteen significant biographies (D12) – 95¢

THE IMITATION OF CHRIST – Thomas à Kempis. Edited with an Introduction by Harold C. Gardiner, S.J. (D17) – 95¢

THE EVERLASTING MAN – G. K. Chesterton (D18) – 95¢

A GRAMMAR OF ASSENT – John Henry Cardinal Newman. Introduction by Étienne Gilson (D19) – $1.45

ST. FRANCIS OF ASSISI – Johannes Jorgensen (D22) – 95¢

ON THE TRUTH OF THE CATHOLIC FAITH (Summa Contra Gentiles) – St. Thomas Aquinas. An Original Image Series:
   Book One: God – Translated by Anton C. Pegis (D26) – $1.25

THE SIGN OF JONAS – Thomas Merton (D31) – $1.25

PARENTS, CHILDREN, AND THE FACTS OF LIFE – Henry V. Sattler, C.SS.R. (D32) – 95¢

SAINT THOMAS AQUINAS – G. K. Chesterton (D36) – 95¢

A HANDBOOK OF THE CATHOLIC FAITH – Dr. N. G. M. Van Doornik, Rev. S. Jelsma, and Rev. De Lisdonk. Edited by Rev. John Greenwood (D38) – $1.65

MARIA CHAPDELAINE – by Louis Hemon. An epic of French-Canadian life (D40) – 75¢

THE STORY OF THE TRAPP FAMILY SINGERS – Maria Augusta Trapp (D46) – 95¢

ST. FRANCIS OF ASSISI – G. K. Chesterton (D50) – 85¢

VIPER'S TANGLE – François Mauriac. A novel of evil and redemption (D51) – 95¢

THE AUTOBIOGRAPHY OF ST. THÉRÈSE OF LISIEUX: The Story of a Soul – Translated by John Beevers. An Image Original (D56) – 85¢

THE GREATEST BIBLE STORIES: A Catholic Anthology from World Literature – Edited by Anne Fremantle (D58) – 85¢

THE CITY OF GOD – St. Augustine. Edited by Vernon J. Bourke. Introduction by Étienne Gilson. Specially abridged (D59) – $1.95

OTHER IMAGE BOOKS

OTHER IMAGE BOOKS